# Out of My Life and Two Visions

2026 The Digital Press @ The University of North Dakota

Library of Congress Control Number: 2026939519
The Digital Press at the University of North Dakota, Grand Forks, North Dakota

ISBN-13: 978-1-966360-14-8 (paperback)
ISBN-13: 978-1-966360-15-5 (Ebook/PDF)

Cover Design: Vitoria Faccin-Herman
Interior Design: William Caraher

# Out of My Life and Two Visions

John Poff

The Digital Press at the University of North Dakota
Grand Forks, ND

# Table of Contents

**Afterwords**

Until you have cried for the fate of every sentient being, you cannot be a real human being.

*There is a through-line in all my writing, from childhood feelings to visions, dreams, poems, experience, prayer...everything, ending up on the back road from Bullhead to Isabel, just above the Grand River, several miles west of Sitting Bull's camp.*

# Introduction

*Paul M. Worley*

In Fall 2021 I had just achieved one of those modest accomplishments you run into as you go through your daily life, the kind of thing you don't set out to do but which nonetheless pops up as an opportunity that strikes you as significant enough that you deviate from whatever supposedly more important things you are working on and do something different, at least for a time. Specifically, after emails and hope and Willian Caraher's infinite patience with me, *NDQ* was moving forward with the republication of some of late-MLB closer Dan Quisenberry's poetry. I loved Quiz's work on the mound as a kid, and encountering his poetic work as an adult was the kind of thing that kept me going during the pandemic. To some extent, the way that project came together reminded me how random and complicated every aspect of existence really is at a moment when the randomness and complications of life were at the forefront of everyone's minds. And so quite randomly, as I drove down the highway from Asheville to work at my now former University, I settled in to listen to *Effectively Wild* episode 1739, the episode that featured none other than the author of the present book, I was probably a little fuller of myself than I had a right to be, and without a doubt more self-confident. I was curious when the hosts said their guest, John Poff, was also a poet, and when he read some of his work on air I immediately resolved to write Ben Lindbergh and see if he could put me in touch with John with the idea that we'd publish some of his work in *NDQ*.

What began as a guy randomly listening to a podcast randomly reaching out to a podcast guest quickly led to thousands of words of correspondence on everything from children to poetry to politics, fewer phone calls than maybe I'd like, and finally, the book you are reading. Many people will pick up this book because it's a fine addition to the canon of baseball literature. It is certainly that but to be clear it is not *just* or *only* baseball literature. The essay Poff is best known for, "Donnie Moore: A Racial Memoir," is one of the best pieces of baseball writing in print, as well as one of the most honest, searing commentaries on race in the United States ever written by a white person, as the author sits uncomfortably with his own complicity within a racialized system of being, tacitly requiring his white readers to do the same.

I wrote the previous words while at work, a few weeks ago. After multiple interruptions I'm back at home, sitting down with a cup of coffee, clearing my head to finish the foreword. I mention this because John and I talk a lot about time and the power of words to *do* and not just describe, and I hope my inserting this anecdote into the foreword will make him laugh (I'm pretty sure it just did). I also bring it up because time dilation like that is a unique power of words, even if it's something of a well worn literary trope, to highlight the fact that, above all else, John Poff is an incredibly talented literary writer in voice, vocabulary, and craft. In my view, as a visionary (and he is very much a visionary), John carries on the proud literary tradition of writers like Blake and Ginsberg, those who dare to see the world as it is, as it REALLY is, and as it COULD be if we simply had the courage. From the perspective of 2026 (and if you get to read this in, say, 3026, look it up, 2026 was a hell of a year) John speaks to something we, particularly those of us in the United States, have lost through the fables we tell ourselves about the country and its founding. Who else, for example, could put together the end of a poem like "Baseball sestina," a poem dedicated to baseball great Enos Slaughter?

There is a park where natives and invaders
smoke the same tobacco,
Where the sound of one hand clapping is
known,
And where the wind blowing and the railroad
whistle are the same.

There it is, a European poetic form that is almost 1000 years old intersecting with Zen koans, baseball, and colonization. And of course, the notion that non-Native readers are not simply colonizers or conquerors, but invaders.

Sit back, share a cup of coffee with me (or not), and read this book. John Poff has things to say. Read. Listen. Make a new friend. It may feel random right now, but I can guarantee that, years from now, and realize you were doing the things you were really meant to do all along.

# Foreword

The heart of this book is the Donnie Moore essay at the beginning of Part I and the Intimations of 2011 essay beginning the second section. I am not sensitive about people thinking it might be presumptuous or overblown to call the events described "visions". It is natural to talk with Lakota people in South Dakota about this, first because the reason I am there and speaking with them at all is the second vision. Also, people there are comfortable with someone saying "I had a vision" to describe the reason for their actions. I am quick to say in those moments I don't think my visions are on the same level in terms of clarity and spiritual depth as the visions of a Lakota holy person.

But they are strong enough for me. I stand by them, as visions, first because they emboldened me to do things in the "real world" I wouldn't otherwise have done. More importantly they are the source of the two basic conclusions I have reached about my life and the times in which I've lived: We totally fail to understand the insidious, all-pervasive ways racism works and acts in my (white) culture, and there is something in Lakota culture the world needs.

I stand, or fall, as well by these two conclusions. If the Donnie Moore essay didn't still hold up, I wouldn't have a book. Unfortunately, it has held up all too well, tragically well. The reason Donald Trump was elected President of the United States was simply that we had a Black President.

I don't see how that can even be a matter for debate. I was teaching high school English to seniors in the years after Obama was elected. In both 2010 and 2011, well into his presidency, I did word association "tests" with those classes. Like a lot of things I did as a teacher, this was partly just for fun, but I admit I was a little sly about it, and over the course of a couple of them I worked in first, George Bush, and then Barack Obama. It was nearly universal "president" for Bush and, with some jittery laughter, unanimously "Black" for Obama. This is not an inconsequential truth.

# *Vision I*

NEW YORK
MASS
PENN
RI
CONN
MD
VIRGINIA
NJ
DELAWARE
NORTH CAROLINA
SOUTH CAROLINA
GEORGIA

## Donnie Moore: A Racial Memoir

In 1989, in the days preceding Donnie Moore's death, I found myself replaying in my mind a small baseball memory from playing against him ten years earlier. Donnie was pitching for Wichita, and I was with Oklahoma City in the American Association. The incident was this: Keith Moreland and I had hit back-to-back home runs in the early innings of a game Donnie Moore started. What I remembered was that we were leading off a later inning, and as we waited in the on-deck circle for warm-ups to end, we were discussing the possibility that he might throw at us in retaliation for the home runs.

That's it. But as I replayed this scenario over and over, it hit me that for all the factors that go into why a pitcher might brush your back, the critical factor in this instance, what made us talk about it as a real possibility, was simply that Donnie Moore was Black. It wasn't the only consideration, but it was the crucial one and I didn't recognize it at the time. Memory can be an incredible filter—the only thing I remember clearly about that day is the discussion with Moreland, and in that new focus I could see an unexpected and subtle racism at work.

I also remembered something that happened the next day. Sometime in the pregame preparation, probably before we took infield practice, Donnie yelled at me across the infield in a good-natured way about the cheap home run I had hit. He was right. Wichita was an incredibly small park, and I had just sort of lofted one over the fence in left center. I remember clearly the smile and the good-natured banter and that I didn't respond easily. I don't know if I even said anything. Partly this was the code—I didn't joke with pitchers on other teams much. But I had played against Donnie for quite awhile and we had a certain respect for each other that made that sort of thing OK. So I'll never know why I couldn't match that smile of his, which is still vivid in my mind. How much was legitimate competitiveness and how much was Black-white misunderstanding, or my being inhibited simply by that previous expectation of being thrown at?

What hit me powerfully was how subtly and yet clearly I had participated in this racism. I didn't feel guilty about it; it's hard not to consider any angle from which a brushback pitch might come. I felt surprised and overwhelmed, but those feelings were mild compared to the way I felt upon driving home from work, turning on the news, and learning that Donnie Moore had shot his wife and killed himself shortly after his career ended.

As eerie as this personal vision was, as much as it shook the hell out of me, I didn't feel touched by the cosmos or as if I were an important part of this tragic scenario. Rather I felt totally buried and powerless by my small participation in an overwhelmingly large evil.

Donnie Moore was an interesting player. I first played against him in 1977. He was in Wichita and I had just joined Oklahoma City. He had been in the big leagues, had a reputation for having good stuff, and was trying to come back from arm problems. What I remembered was that he had ripped the Cubs' management in an article in *The Sporting News* about the way he was being treated. I remember thinking it was unusual for a ballplayer to make waves when he was hurt. I believe there were a lot of associations attached to players in the minor leagues who openly criticized management, and it could be a definite racial situation. First of all, it took a certain audacity for any minor leaguer to speak up because minor league players were so powerless. But I think it worked racially this way: a white player who criticized management could be a troublemaker, or he could be trying to get traded, or he could just be a character—a flake. A Black player who criticized management was viewed simply as a troublemaker. Donnie may have been one but all I can remember now is that friendly smile. He was also a "black" Black player. That is, his features were dark and he could look imposing. In my generation of athletes, white ballplayers could react negatively or be intimidated by something as simple as that. It was almost certainly a factor for me in considering the prospect of him throwing at us.

Donnie's great success as a relief pitcher in the American League surprised me a little bit—I didn't think his stuff was *that* good—but in the years after I quit playing I was happy to see him doing so well. He is remembered now primarily as the guy that lost the playoffs for the Angels one year by serving up a home run to Dave Henderson. Supposedly that experience contributed to his problems that wound up in tragedy. I wouldn't doubt it, but the way I felt the night he died was that the crucial X factor that tipped the scales was our society's subtle and pervasive racism. Ex-ballplayers have a hard time adjusting to the end of their careers. This is not a flippant statement—divorce, suicide, and substance abuse problems are tremendous. But when I think about how Donnie Moore was looked at throughout his career, how Black athletes and Black people are viewed in this society, I felt this tragedy was simply another perverse triumph for racism.

Donnie Moore died eight years after my career ended, and when I walked out in my backyard after learning the news of his death, I realized I had still been waiting for some final shoe to drop in understanding or feeling reconciled about my experiences in baseball. My career in baseball *was* frustrating. I wanted and felt I deserved a lot more time in the big leagues. Although I never questioned my decision to quit, I realized I had that great American yearning for catharsis, some final reconciliation and acceptance and understanding about the way things had turned out.

What I felt was that this tragedy was that catharsis, that it was the closing of my baseball experience but in a terrible, helpless, bitter way. All this struggle for personal success and understanding was being waged in a meaningless ocean, meaningless because the larger evil was being so inadequately addressed.

There is a certain kind of old-timer who, if you talk to him long enough, will tell you what is the one thing that "ruined this country." I am a collector of these statements, such as "Drugs ruined this country," or "Unions ruined this country," or in the

‘60’s, in my hometown at least, it wasn’t uncommon to hear people say “The Beatles ruined this country.” My personal favorite came from an old cowboy I met in New Mexico in 1975 who told me that “Barbed wire ruined this country,” by which he meant, of course, the beautiful Southwest. In that same way, I could address the problems of baseball and say that in my opinion Astroturf ruined baseball, or amphetamines, or the ridiculous way we idolize ballplayers. But the horrible truth is that racism ruined this country, has been ruining it for 500 years, and it is racism that ruined baseball—ruins it still, I believe, because we don’t acknowledge what has happened, or work at really changing it.

This is the racial history of baseball: for the first 50 years of this century Major League Baseball practiced *apartheid.* The obligatory comment, it seems to me, is that this is not surprising given the nature of American society then, although I don’t know how long we can continue to plead generational ignorance. After all, it is a former slave trader who wrote “Amazing Grace”. In the 1820’s, as a teenager, Abraham Lincoln could debate in all seriousness the question: “Who has a greater right to complain, the Indian or the Negro?” and yet somehow it is applying a late twentieth-century mentality to a fundamentally different age to suggest, for instance, that the great Gehrig might have sat out just one of those 2130 games to protest baseball's racism.

At any rate, then Jackie Robinson came along, and white America has been patting itself on the back ever since, as if his career was a triumph for *us*. This is a problem for white people: We judge our level of racism by what Black people achieve. I think in looking at the racial history of baseball, we need to separate the achievements of Black athletes from the attitudes of white America. I would argue that that the racial story of the last 40 years of Major League Baseball is that American society has consistently failed to wake up to the implications of Black athletes' achievements, in effect has consistently failed to learn what it means to be nonracist.

I want to make this point by focusing on a few Black players in the 50's and 60's, the decades immediately after Jackie Robinson broke the color barrier. I believe that because we didn't respond to the larger implications of what these players' careers meant, we completely missed an opportunity to confront and purify our racial past.

Look at it this way: When Jackie Robinson's splendid career began to kick in, if white society had not been racist at its heart, one would expect some general feeling of appreciation for and curiosity about the great Black players of the preceding decades. But as if Jackie Robinson weren't enough, it seems ironic that as soon as the barriers were dropped, two of the greatest players of any generation or color—Willie Mays and Henry Aaron—began their tremendous, remarkably long and consistent careers.

It is one thing to drop a specific racial barrier. It is another to respond to the implications of the achievements Black athletes made when allowed to compete evenly. It seems to me that the implication of the '50's was that the odds were very strong that baseball fans had missed a lot by largely missing the careers of players like Josh Gibson, Judy Johnson, and Satchel Paige. An appropriate response would have been to immediately rehabilitate the reputations of these great athletes—have them on talk shows, induct them into the Hall of Fame, etc.

What actually happened? Almost exactly the opposite. I grew up in the 50's and 60's as a fan of baseball history and I feel in retrospect that I was propagandized by a racial myth. The myth was that the old-time players were better than modern-day players. It was easy to buy into on the basis of statistics because of the overwhelming shadow of Babe Ruth and the inflated lifetime averages of old ballplayers. The fact is that the white major league could not possibly have been quality baseball by modern-day standards, if only on the basis of the absence then of Black (and Latin American) players who are now playing in relatively large numbers.

It's not just that this myth has been propagated and adhered to religiously, but that in my opinion it was created directly out of and fueled by blatant racism. I used to wonder as a child why adults were so adamant about the superiority of players in the old days. It was an article of faith, a point of vital importance, and I have no doubt that racism, conscious and unconscious, was the driving force behind it.

In a bizarre sort of way, I think Roger Maris was victimized by this racism. The frenzied pressure to put an asterisk beside his home run record was primarily an attempt to sanctify the old, segregated Major League. The fact is that it would be more just and accurate to put an asterisk beside any record still standing which was achieved during the period of baseball *apartheid*. I regret having to say that. To me the greatest record in all of sports is Joe DiMaggio's 56-game hitting streak, but it is sadly cheapened because there was not even the possibility he would have to face Satchel Paige during the course of it. Not that Paige would necessarily have stopped him. Personally, I prefer to think it's likelier that the Indians would have had a more offensively-oriented third baseman than Ken Keltner—a Bill Madlock type, for instance—who might not have handled DiMaggio's hot shots in that memorable 57th game. That would mean, given DiMaggio's ensuing 17-game hitting streak, that the record would now stand at an almost unthinkable seventy-four games.

Of course it would also mean we live in a different universe. The point here, I think, is that while it's easy to criticize modern players on almost any standard of judgment, they at least have the fundamental integrity to play against any other players that can earn the opportunity.

So we slept through the "implications" of the careers of Jackie Robinson, Hank Aaron, and Willie Mays. Indeed, we actively tried to subvert and deny these implications. In the 60's, the most important players, in my opinion, were Bob Gibson and Frank Robinson. The importance of their careers is not just their greatness on the field but that they shattered, through the nature of their performance, the most devastating stereotypes then current about

Black athletes. These stereotypes included notions that Black athletes were gifted physically but less able to handle the pressures of competition, to be winners or leaders, to "grind it out", etc.

Gibson and Robinson were dominant not only because of their great baseball skills (talents which, I would also point out, had nothing to do with either foot speed or jumping ability) but also because of their competitiveness, their ability to win, their sense of purpose about playing. They were in effect the perfect "white" ballplayers of their time—"white" meaning of course some combination of attributes not properly associated with race.

When I was playing, stories that filtered down to the minor leagues about great players had a very short half-life. In the mid-70's, it was rare to hear much even about players from just the previous decade. I remember Claude Osteen telling me in 1976 that the most amazing thing about watching Sandy Koufax pitch was the way Koufax would bear down to prevent a run from scoring on those rare occasions when the lead-off batter in an inning would hit a triple. Freddie Beene was so adamant about the play of Paul Blair in center field—he was the best there ever was or could be—that he made a believer out of me though I never saw Blair play a single game. But stories about Gibson's competitiveness were legion, covering everything from his demeanor on the mound to how uncomfortable hitters on opposing teams felt simply riding in a hotel elevator with him.

It wasn't only Gibson and Robinson, of course. Ferguson Jenkins, Lou Brock, Bill White, and many others shattered stereotypes in one way or another. Had the implications of these achievements sunk in, or been accepted openly, I believe baseball would have changed both dramatically and subtly. Dramatic changes would have included moves to place Black people in management, not just field manager positions but also as general managers, where the real power lies. Subtle changes would have included the rise of Black players in utility (reserve) positions and seeking out and signing Black pitchers on the same basis as white pitchers. Even today, a Black pitcher is far likelier to have greater physical talent, greater "stuff," than his white counterpart. I think the idea that a Black pitcher can not be smart or crafty or gifted competitively has been endemic in major league organizations for forty years.

A few years ago it became a media event when two Black managers, Frank Robinson and Cito Gaston, opposed each other for the first time in the history of the Major Leagues. I would guess that for Robinson this kind of attention was most insulting. If nothing else besides his own career in baseball had resonated with white people, Black managers would have been a non-issue before the end of the 60's. As it turned out in the 90's, he had to wade through stereotypes about Blacks in management, just like he had to wade through stereotypes about the competitive abilities of Black athletes in the 60's.

Indeed, it seems apparent that this sort of pattern happens over and over for Black players in baseball. Henry Aaron's career was an important and timely statement about what had been missing when baseball was segregated, and yet as he approached Babe Ruth's all-time home run record, he received endless and frankly racist abuse from baseball "fans" who were clinging to their notions of white superiority in baseball.

The 70's were my decade in professional baseball, and here my discussion becomes personal. What do I remember? I remember that the consciousness of race pervaded everything in a professional baseball locker room. If you played with or against Black ballplayers, you became friends possibly, and you possibly shared concerns, values, dope, and yet in all your conversations there was the ongoing subliminal buzz—you're Black, you're Black, you're Black. I remember thinking there should have been a *Saturday Night Live* sketch with Gilda Radner bringing home a Black boyfriend who was impeccable—Harvard Medical School, perfect family, and so forth—and with the Bill Murray parent, at the end of each incredible accomplishment, saying simply: "You're Black, you're Black, you're Black", because that has been the ongoing chant all my life. And often it has been the audible, conscious chant. In professional baseball locker rooms in the 70's, there would usually be a few Black ballplayers on each team, and for many white players in a typical conversation with a Black ballplayer there was what might be called the racial reference time bomb, so that every two minutes, or five minutes, or whatever, the white player's conversation would rise to the inevitable, "and then you got your black ass outta there", or "dadadada, dadadada — your black ass". In the early 70's, there seemed to be a certain newness to this kind of dialogue between the races and when the Black player would respond with some sort of racial comment, acceptance of the joke, the feeling of relief that swept through the room was palpable, like a mitigation of guilt for the white people. How many times have I heard a white person say, "I don't have any trouble with Black people. We joke about it all the time." Joke about what?

Was this consciousness of race fundamental to the experience of playing professional baseball in the 70's? Much of the ephemera from that time has fallen from me completely: the cheap motel rooms, the bus rides, also, sadly, many of the friendships, and even, in large part, the feeling of hitting a home run. But that racial awareness is with me daily. Last year I coached my son's Little League team and one of the parents introduced himself to me as a professor at the University of Colorado. I asked his teaching area, and when he responded "Aeronautical Engineering", I'll never know how much of my enthusiastic "Oh really" was related to the fact he was the first rocket scientist I ever met and how much was related to my tacit assumption that he was teaching in a Black studies program, or at least somewhere in the humanities. But one thing is certain: it was a moment that connected me instantly with sitting next to Lonnie Smith or Bobby Brown in the Oklahoma City clubhouse in, say, 1978.

I am terrible at golf and admit it freely. In a lifetime of playing occasional rounds on the kind of cheap nine-hole courses where my game belongs, it has been my hope to become a bogey golfer. At some point it hit me that if I made one good shot on a hole, I would make bogey, but also that I would get the same score with one bad shot. In my experience in this country, there was a time when many a dyed-in-the-wool racist would have some insight that he was wrong, that Black people were not intrinsically worthless or even unusual, and this would feel like progress. But now I am much more conscious of how revealing the one mistake is. I have sat in on more conversations than I can count with white and Black people where we seem to be doing great, where there is a real focus on our mutual humanity, until the great welling up—"You're Black"—comes out and I think we are still making bogeys. I think this because I have seen the look of resignation and disgust on Black faces when the seemingly innocent racial remark is made. I have been the cause of that look more than once, even in those years when I literally fought, verbally, to be the most liberal person in the room.

Does anyone remember the enormous furor Andrew Young aroused when, as U.S. delegate to the United Nations, he proclaimed that "We are all racists". The public outcry was tremendous. I believe the year was 1977. The Carter presidency, which I had high hopes for, was already in trouble and I remember thinking, baseball-style, "Are these guys trying, or what?" The next day I caught a brief soundbite of Andrew Young commenting on the uproar he had created. The reporters caught up with him at a New York airport, just arriving or departing, and he said something like, "What I meant is that we are all of us, in this century, tinged with the consciousness of race."

That really struck a chord with me. It was a turning point in my own consciousness about racism and I began to see things in a different way. I began to acknowledge and understand that racism I had felt and expressed in the world, and I became less anxious to participate in that great liberal competition to be the least racist person in the room. In fact, I began to think that wasn't the solution but simply another expression of the problem.

The real heart of my eight-season playing career was the years 1978 and 1979, which I spent mostly in Oklahoma City at the Triple A level. As I recall, we had two Black players on the team: Bobby Brown and Lonnie Smith. Bobby was, for white people, the prototypical "I don't use this word in regard to race, but this guy is a nigger" Black person. People really used to say that. Bobby could in fact drive anyone crazy, could talk beyond the point of all talking, until he became a walking argument for gun control. Roger Freed was the same way. If there's anything I don't know about Roger's life before 1980, it's only because I've forgotten it. I genuinely liked both of them, but at some point over the course of a long season, if I'd had a gun in my locker, I would have shot them both. The difference is that I never heard anyone call Roger Freed a nigger.

Bobby was a remarkable athlete. He was 6'2", 195 lbs. or so, and very fast. He stole fifty or sixty bases in Triple A and hit .300. He ran flatfooted, really without much grace, and hit first base like a ton of bricks. I remember thinking it would break my ankle to land on first like that, although I was larger and actually stronger in some ways than him. I noticed he had really big hands and feet. Somewhere along the line, noticing his hands and feet, that flatfooted running style, his jokes about his home in Virginia, it hit me that there were people, maybe even then, who would have referred to Bobby as a "field nigger". In thinking this, and remembering Andrew Young, and beginning to understand the way we are all embroiled in this murky swamp of race consciousness, I began to wonder: Is this what other people think, or is this what I think?

If Bobby Brown was the prototypical nigger, Lonnie Smith was the atypical nigger. His entire demeanor, I believe, was nonstereotypical. This doesn't mean he wasn't stereotyped. Quite the contrary. He was stereotyped as a strange nigger. To me, Lonnie was naturally thoughtful, cool, and even gentle. White people never knew what to make of this. I believe that consequently a great deal of pressure built up inside him. I know that once a season or so Lonnie would snap during a game. One night in Oklahoma City he was called out on what appeared to me to be a questionable but not outrageously bad call. Lonnie went crazy with the umpire for a few seconds, pulled second base out of the ground, sat down with it in the outfield grass, and wouldn't give it back. Even then I thought there was a little more going on than a bad call. When he hit a home run in the playoffs a couple years ago for Atlanta and circled the bases swearing and gesticulating vigorously, I wasn't surprised.

But the primo, all-American, top-of-the-line "I've got nothing against Black people, but this guy is a nigger" for the 70's was Mickey Rivers. Rivers played for the Yankees in the late 70's and was on national television frequently. I believe everyone in America who watched baseball in the 70's saw Mickey Rivers hit a foul ball down the right field line, run it out 3/4 of the way, and then have to return to home plate. Rather than jogging back, he did the Mickey Rivers' pigeon-toed, slow, ambling walk. It was a strange combination of Step-N-Fetchit shuffling, and the slow, frightening, powerful walk of Jimmy Brown returning to the huddle. I think it hit white America just that way, filling us literally with both fear and loathing. All across America, in living rooms and bars and basements, white people were moved to comment: "Would you look at that nigger!" I know this because I heard it countless times myself. I have no idea what it's like to be called a nigger, but I surely know every way there is to call Mickey Rivers a nigger. My understanding is that the continent groans under the weight of this.

Yo
America
Mickey Rivers
Was not a nigger

My favorite player in the 70's was Jerry Manuel. When I was growing up in Findlay, Ohio, we had a great high school baseball player named Clay Bryson. He was in my mother's American history class, and one summer we became friends, though I was several years younger than him. One night my parents and I drove over to Pemberville to watch an American Legion game. Clay's position was center field and in the warm-ups between innings, he threw the ball to the other outfielders with such grace and fluid movements that my mother couldn't stop laughing and exclaiming over it. That's how I felt about Jerry Manuel, who was a second baseman and shortstop for several years in the American Association when I played there. He had the greatest, softest hands I ever saw, and he was the only player that could get me out of the clubhouse to watch the opposing team take infield practice.

I always thought he was the perfect utility player for a big league team and I always wondered, because Black reserves were uncommon, if he got as much time in the Major Leagues as he deserved. He was fiercely competitive, yet with a wonderful team attitude. He even had some pop in his bat. He also fit the mold for a utility infielder in a slightly negative way. Like most reserve infielders, he did not have tremendous speed. Black middle infielders in the 70's who were not extremely fast were pretty rare.

There is an interesting aspect to Jerry Manuel's career today. His name is bandied about occasionally as a candidate for a managerial job. While it probably wouldn't be heralded as such, this would be a real breakthrough. Except for the NBA, Black managers or head coaches have almost universally been former great players or large, imposing men, or both. I am thinking of Art Shell and Dennis Green in the NFL, Frank Robinson, Cito Gaston, and Don Baylor in the big leagues, and John Thompson, George Raveling, and Nolan Richardson in college basketball. We seem to want a Black man to have real heft before we turn a team over to him. This is a strange standard for baseball, where the best managers usually come from the ranks of former players who survived as much by craft and desire as by physical talent. It would be most ironic if Manuel's relative lack of playing time in the big leagues kept him from getting a managing position. As with Robinson and Aaron, it would be another example of a Black athlete having to jump through the same sorts of hoops decade after decade.

I want to close my discussion of baseball in the 70's with a few words about the Major League Players' Association, the baseball players' union. When Al Campanis got befuddled on "Nightline" a few years ago and let his hair down to reveal the depth and ignorance of his racial stereotyping, an inquiry was launched into the absence of Blacks in management positions and a few changes were made. A couple of questions needed to be asked. Why weren't people concerned about this earlier?

More to the point, why hadn't the Players' Association, which should have had a philosophical and practical interest in the problem, already done something about it?

The history of the Baseball Players' Association over the last twenty-five years is strange and fascinating. It's strange, in my view, because a real union wound up creating a whole generation of committed, trickle-down theory capitalists. It is fascinating because Marvin Miller was such a brilliant guy and he commanded the absolute loyalty and respect of Major League ballplayers.

I was in four Major League spring training camps. Every year Marvin and his assistant, Don Fehr, would meet with each team for an hour or so to explain and discuss the issues facing the union. I should say "issue", because it was always just the one thing: free agency and the owners' efforts to stop it.

I thought Marvin was incredible. I walked into my first meeting with much of the same skepticism about the Players' Association that the rest of America had. I walked out an hour later humming Woody Guthrie tunes. I marveled at this because I never thought of myself as easily proselytized. I marveled even more because while I was sort of a goofy ex-English major from Duke, two other young players—Lonnie Smith, an African-American from Compton, and Keith Moreland, a former University of Texas Longhorn in the days when that still meant something—were humming the same tunes. In 1980, I asked Dave Rader how he felt about the probable upcoming strike (which was delayed until 1981). He looked directly at me and said, "I owe everything I have to Marvin. I'll do whatever he wants."

This is not to say that Marvin dictated to the Union. His brilliance lay in explaining both the issues and the options facing the Association. His speeches should have been taped. He was clear and thorough and never condescending. He actively solicited the players' views.

The problem was the Association felt so threatened by the owners' assault on free agency that other issued were never discussed. I remember Marvin saying explicitly that, unfortunately, other issues had to be put on the back burner. Still, at the end of every meeting I attended, he asked openly if players had any other topics to bring up. If I can fault Lou Gehrig for not protesting baseball's racism, I fault myself, though a fringe player at best, even more for not saying in 1978, or 1979, or 1980, or 1981, "Why don't we say we'll strike if the owners don't agree to hire some Black, or minority, general managers?" Why didn't I do this? I didn't have the vision to frame the question. If I had, I probably wouldn't have had the courage to speak it out. I've never met anyone before or since like Marvin Miller, but I don't know how he sleeps at night. Of course, I am up quite late myself tonight, writing this.

I can't say very much about racism and baseball in the 80's, partly because I am no longer close to the sport and partly because, as I feel we missed so many chances to wake up in the past few decades, the Black athlete in baseball is now little more than a hired hand. He may be a respected hired hand, like Dave Stewart, or he may be viewed stereotypically as a gifted athlete who doesn't have the right attitude, like Rickey Henderson, but either way he's a hired hand. For me, though our language may have changed slightly, Rickey Henderson was the nigger of the 80's, in the eyes of white America, as surely as Mickey Rivers was the nigger of the 70's. Our preoccupation with false "events", like the occasional hiring of a Black manager, only illustrated how far we didn't come.

There were a couple sports items in the 80's, at least in my opinion, that were noteworthy. One is the story of Michael Jordan. I believe white America glommed onto Michael Jordan for two reasons.

One is we were intoxicated by his incredible athleticism. The other is we were scared to death of it. I don't think the millions of dollars Jordan received in endorsement money reflected simply his ability to sell shoes. I honestly believe the advertising companies were guided by the unconscious will of white Americans to buy Jordan off, to make him tame, scrutable, and one of us. White America truly wanted to love Michael Jordan and if it took twenty-six million dollars a year to make certain he was one of our own, then so be it.

To me, our effort to adopt Michael Jordan, or whiticize him, was very much like our effort to adopt Michael Jackson. The difference between the two, in my mind, is that Michael Jackson didn't have the family background to withstand the onslaught, and thus his descent into whatever kind of world it is in which he now lives.

Jordan is different. I admire him enormously for his baseball experiment. Like most ballplayers, especially ex-ballplayers, I feel a little threatened when a great athlete from another sport takes up baseball in a seemingly cavalier fashion. It just isn't that easy. Jordan is discovering that, and yet staying with it.

He has already paid a price. A year ago, most basketball fans viewed him as unquestionably the greatest player of all time. Because the Bulls did so well this year without him and because at the moment he is a mediocre minor-leaguer, I think many people are re-evaluating that assessment.

There seems to be a consensus now that playing baseball is Jordan's way of mourning his father. I would put it differently. I believe that by turning his back on the money and, especially, the adulation, and staying with baseball as he has, he is paying his father the greatest possible tribute. He is showing that he has the strength not to buckle.

The other interesting thing to me about the 80's was the growing preoccupation of white America with Black superiority in sports. This culminated with, and was legitimized by, a "news" special hosted by Tom Brokaw inquiring into the phenomenon.

I don't think it's too hard to see where we are going with this. I believe we want to establish a genetic basis for the success of Black athletes. This is a two-fold agenda. First, it dehumanizes Blacks, emphasizing their physicality. Secondly, while surveys show that half of us at any given moment don't know who the Vice President is, or when World War II ended, it seems to me that almost all white people are aware we outperform Blacks on IQ tests. I think we have a trade in mind. We will give Black people an inherent physical superiority, which both demeans them and gives us a good excuse for not being able to dunk, while we retain for ourselves an innate intellectual superiority. Incidentally, I do think it is possible to inquire in a less racist way into the success of Black athletes, but that's a subject for another essay. I'll give you a hint: It's not genetic and white people don't come off too well.

Certainly it's early to draw conclusions about racism in the 90's, but in the seeds of the Michael Jordan phenomenon and the rise of a Black middle class, I think it's clear where we are going. Personally, I believe our racist agenda will be to isolate the Black middle class from the rest of the Black community, rendering the middle class powerless and making the rest of the Black community easy to hate and repress. Let's face it: this is brilliant. I look at this picture over and over again and I can't decide if it is driven by our conscious or unconscious will, but after 500 years of always selecting the best possible way to hold onto our racism, what difference does it make?

I'll close here with one last note about baseball and racism. I don't presume to have any more insight into the real sources of racism than anyone else blundering through the last years of this century. But I would say this: Picture Little League teams composed respectively of white kids, Black kids, Mexican kids, and any other culture with which you are familiar. Imagine a game where the best player on each team goes 0-4, the worst player goes 4-4, and the team wins. How does the best player on each team feel? Those of us who are white know how the white kid feels. This is a white thing, and I don't think it is idealizing other cultures to say they are different. Kids everywhere are capable of meanness, pettiness, and individual jealousy, but to be successful and feel threatened by someone else's success, to feel in fact a terrible loneliness and fear in the face of someone else's success—for me, that feeling is unique to our culture. For me, also, this is the concrete heart of racism, and the fact I have had to come to grips with is that I have seen and felt this most clearly and personally on a ball field.

## Baseball Dream

The first summer I played in the Cape Cod League, after my sophomore year in college, I drove a fruit truck for Chris Decas—the Decas Brothers, Inc.—leaving Wareham, "The Gateway to the Cape", by 6:00 or 6:30 and making the rounds to stores and restaurants out to Falmouth and occasionally Hyannis, back to the warehouse by 2:00.

He had three trucks and a van, and a semi that went up to Boston early every day to get the day's produce. Marshall drove the semi and helped us load the trucks before heading home, finished for the day, having had such an early start. He was a pretty cool guy, mid-30's, African-American. His girlfriend's name was stenciled on the driver-side door of the truck. He said one of the most spontaneously funny things I've ever heard. The radio was playing some kind of early-morning farm report, reading out the daily prices as we're walking together to the cooler to get more stuff, and it sounds unmistakably like the news guy says, "And the price of cock today is 89 cents a pound." Without missing a beat Marshall said: "Let's see, I've got five pounds so for me that would be about… "

This was the dream I had one night that summer: Marshall was standing at the edge of a swamp. On the other side were three figures, all sitting down. I immediately recognized two of them. In the middle was God, really strong older male, middle 50's maybe, serenity and power in his face. To God's right was Jesus, not yet 30, by my estimation, perfect, of course, but not just in my memory, also clearly at that dreaming moment emanating a sense of, really: What is this guy for? And then on the other side of God was a very old man, weeping.

Marshall seemed to be weighing trying to get across the swamp. From my vantage as the dreamer, it looked like a very bad decision, but he went for it, getting bogged down hopelessly not even halfway across, flailing, the old man weeping. A snake rose up out of the swamp beside Marshall, obviously preparing to strike at his neck—a death blow—a moment so intense it woke me up.

This has been the standard for me all my life of a dream that was, as I have said elsewhere, qualitatively different from the rest of my dreaming life. Unlike nearly all my other dreams, it has never faded from memory, although I don't remember sharing it with anyone for nearly 50 years.

## Baseball Sestina

An old ballplayer broke off a plug of
tobacco
And said, "When you get to the ballpark,
Check which way the wind is blowing,
And then get yourself a good ball to hit." I
took that native
Advice to heart, but it was years before I
felt it in my hands.
You see, I rode the bus; he took the
railroad.

The ocean is a whale-highway, but
America is a railroad.
Many times I've crossed it, rolling my own
tobacco
Into homemade cigarettes, cupping there
in my hand
The eternal promise of addiction, a park
That's beautiful, filled with hope and
native
Flowers, but always just around some
corner, blowing

Out of reach like this smoke is blowing
Across the continent. At ten I played ball
down by the railroad.
The leather and dirt and grass and wood
provided a native
Thrill. My dad sat in the stands smoking
tobacco.
Did his thoughts ever run out past the
parked
Cars, out to a whole world he once hoped
to hold in his hand?

Once I hit a home run and the audience
gave me a hand.
As I circled the bases, I felt the wind
blowing
Across my every molecule. This was a new
park
To be in, fantastic, like a railroad
To the sky. When original Americans
smoked tobacco,
America was like this, something
tremendous, a native

Splendor. That first home run is with me
    yet, a nativity
Scene enshrined in memory. If my
    wrinkled, weathered hands
Now shake, still I remember. Pass the
    tobacco.
Sometimes I think what was once me is
    now blowing
Far off, on the other side of the railroad
Where we used to play. A graveyard is also
    a park.

We drove all night to get to Cleveland and
    parked
Six blocks from the stadium. The natives
Rushed to sell us junk and we felt
    railroaded
By the ticket-takers. Still, through the
    prism of clapping hands,
I see myself there, one moment real, one
    moment blowing
Into nothingness, like a dream of Indian
    tobacco.

There is a park where natives and invaders
    smoke the same tobacco,
Where the sound of one hand clapping is
    known,
And where the wind blowing and the
    railroad whistle are the same.

## Experience: Amphetamine Story

What is that feeling when you are twenty-two years old and in love and you are heading off to Mexico to play ball (until two weeks ago you didn't even know they played professional baseball in Mexico) and you are in love with Patti and it is her funky red van you are riding in and, honestly, the road unfolds like a ribbon to—what? Not Oz or Valhalla for me but just the hope of washing up, like Odysseus, on some distant shore, not older or wiser or better but just—alive and different. Maybe nameless.

Who can't see themselves in hopeful, pristine moments—as simple as a first apartment or a new love affair, and who can't see that fundamental yearning for what it really is: the hope of losing oneself totally—the lackluster culture, family conditioning, the teachers and ministers and doctors droning on and on until all unwilling we wear that droning as ourselves.

At any rate, this was what I was thinking and feeling in the fall of '74 when I returned to the old hometown—Findlay, Ohio—to pick up Patti and begin our life of living together by driving down to Mazatlan for the winter. We packed up the van and stopped at a travel agency for maps and information about passports. There was no particular reason for them to be helpful to us—we weren't buying anything—but they were helpful, telling us how to get passports at the border and so forth. They seemed to smile a lot to themselves. They must have been amused by our innocence and stupidity: "Now just exactly where is Mexico, anyhow?" But what did we care? And what did they know about Mexico, anyhow, except what they learned at some seminar up in Toledo? Hot damn! We were the ones who would be out there doing it while they were sitting on their fat butts in beautiful downtown Findlay, envisioning a brochure Mexico in the same way they envisioned a brochure Tahiti or Jamaica.

We stepped out of that travel agency and we were in the heart of Findlay (we had both lived there most of our lives), right at the corner newsstand where we had probably bumped into each other, or just missed each other, a hundred times, and with the First National Bank across the street. It was late afternoon. Patti looked strange and vibrant in a suede jacket with fringes in the back and black pants. It seemed like the perfect outfit to wear to Mexico. We had always thought of Findlay as a kind of graveyard—a killing jar for teenage hopes and desires—but today it felt like a launching pad. We stood on that old familiar street corner, in the late afternoon of a late November day, smiling and looking around and waiting for...what? Maybe we hoped old man Herrick, who sold us our first bikes before being run out of business for exposing himself in the back of the shop, would stroll by and wave goodbye to us. Or maybe we hoped our dead mothers would reappear to give us a proper sendoff. Or maybe the moment was enough just as it was.

Where is Mexico? We found it hard to find. We headed south and then west and then south again until I thought of my old friend Guy who lived somewhere close to New Orleans. We went three hundred miles out of our way to see him, with no advance notice. (Actually, six hundred miles out of the way. I had planned to take the southern route to Mazatlan until the van broke down in Del Rio, at the border, and I learned in casual conversation, there is no southern route to Mazatlan. So it was up to El Paso and then over.) We called Guy when we got to town—found his number in the phone book—and miraculously he answered. Grab your girl, Guy, and let's go get drunk.

Honky-tonking it outside New Orleans: a near fight over a pool game. Guy put his glasses down on the edge of the table and looked up at the other guy with a gaze that was instantly and clearly connected to his longtime heritage of good ol' boy insanity and violence: "Now I am telling you, boy, that this is our quarter and it is our turn to shoot pool at this table." The other guy backed down and the evening moved forward.

Lynn, his girlfriend, has short hair, large hips, and is friendly in that way you can almost instantly recognize: she has been lonely all her life. She is the girl sitting by herself in the school cafeteria, writing in her notebook, and not about who she likes or a school assignment. I had never had the patience or the charm to learn just what she was writing about and now, like Keats with poetry, I am surprised and delighted my friend has hooked up with her.

At one point she is playing pinball and we walk up behind her and Guy scopes her hips, framing them like a picture, and his entire body moves in a rhythmic spasm like a good-natured snake, and I am remembering the way he rhapsodized about women with large butts, and this moment connects with every other moment in my life when I've heard men express their feelings about some aspect of a woman's shape. But this is the bedrock—my good friend in love with a lonely woman's hips and expressing it here in this Delta honky-tonk.

Southern chivalry is not dead. Guy insisted on paying for our motel room that night. Somehow we wound up on the east side of the river. I had crossed the Mississippi once or twice before, but that next morning I felt it for the first time: the lumbar vertebrae of America's great water spine—fluid and oppressive...

Three years later, in late August, I was back in New Orleans, finishing out my first season at the Triple A level in the minor leagues. Three years can be a lifetime for a ballplayer. I had been a suspect and then a prospect and then a suspect again and now, with a good season with the Oklahoma City 89ers under my belt, was once more a reasonably legitimate prospect with a reasonably legitimate shot at making the big leagues before too long.

We sort of skidded into New Orleans for the final three-game series of the season, with no game scheduled for our first night in town. There are very few off-days in a Triple A season, maybe four or five in the five months of playing games. In the lower minor leagues, there is only one off-day in the entire 144-game season. That is the day of the Major League All-Star Game, as if all the minor leaguers, on their one off-night in a long season, will try to pick up some pointers from the big leaguers on TV instead of going out and getting drunk and trying to get laid.

So you can see that the combination of being near the end of the season and having an off-night and being in New Orleans tended to create a fairly festive atmosphere among the 89ers. We weren't in downtown New Orleans but there were plenty of bars where we were and they stayed open a hell of a lot later than the bars in Des Moines or Springfield or most of the other cities in the American Association.

Several of us wound up at Rudy's, a place with a circular bar and raised dance floor. I found myself in the kind of drinking party that more than satisfied my humble standards: plenty of time, friendly teammates, and cold beer. To my left were Gary "The Bear" Wilhelm and Rob Crandall. They were both southern boys (in the mid 70's that still meant something) but I never held that against them, especially when we drank beer together. The Bear had been a pitcher at North Carolina a year or two before I played at Duke. He was from Mt. Airy and mainly wanted to make enough money in baseball to be able to go back home and raise hogs. Patti and I had spent the last couple winters in New Mexico, where we had been overpowered by the sunsets and beauty of the landscape, and mainly wanted to make enough money to be able to go back to New Mexico and buy some land where we could smoke dope and look at the sky.

It was a connection of sorts and made for a pretty good conversation, although the three of us tended to wind up on different tracks. I might start in with something about finding a nice piece of land, maybe continuing a conversation that had begun two or three weeks earlier in some late night motel room. The Bear could get behind that idea, but Crandall had hunting dogs and it is my experience that if you drink with someone who has hunting dogs and mention the word "country", sooner or later you are going to be talking hunting stories. This was alright with The Bear—it was part of the life—but the closest I ever came to a hunting experience was the time I was 11 years old and shot a rifle on the target range at Camp Nelson Dodd. When my target sheet came back, I was a cool 0-10. I don't mean for the bull's-eye or even the circles, but for the whole piece of paper. I had hit .567 that summer in Little League. My interests stayed with baseball, and I stayed on the fringe of hunting stories.

It's not easy to write ballplayer dialogue. You run the risk of sounding like a modern-day James Fenimore Cooper. It's not Elmore Leonard dialogue, which is terrific, I think, and realistic because it combines two ideas in one sentence and leaves words out like real people do ("The fuck you wanna do is shoot the little fucker." I mean, who hasn't said that?). For a ballplayer, the pregame preparation and the game and the postgame stuff, even if it involves drinking a lot of beer, are all connected, and this feeling of connectedness influences your conversation, probably for the worse. The thrill of great dialogue for me is the way it captures and identifies, even isolates, the newly created reality in each moment.

Baseball is different. How you do in a game is connected to what you did before the game, and each game is connected to the last, going back all the way to the first time you stepped on a ball field. I coach my son's Little League team and I tried to explain this to them once because they are absolutely clueless. "You know, it's not like a groundball is just hit to you and either you catch it or you don't. You start catching that groundball about two in the afternoon, the way you're thinking and getting ready for the game. You start getting your base hits the night before, and if any of you ever make it to the big leagues, it's probably gonna be because you're grandfathers started making the right preparations." They look at me like I'm crazy.

I remember when Al Oerter announced his decision not to compete in a fifth straight Olympics, about two years before the next Olympics were scheduled. It wasn't because of his age, or because he wanted to go out on top, but because he didn't want to keep making the preparations. He said something like, "If I want to take my family to the beach for a day, even now two years before the Olympics, I've got to think about my training and the effect of the waves on my body. I don't want to do that anymore." I remember thinking that was incredible, unbelievable, and then a few years later I started to understand baseball, and it made perfect sense.

Mark Twain understood this when he learned about the Mississippi River. It was impossible to learn the whole river (as impossible as it is to be completely focused on every pitch in a minor league season, taking into account everything that has ever happened to you on a ball field, and the pitcher's options, and the count, and the angle of the moonrise) but he did it, and then he even wrote about it clearly. Intellectually, Twain was a great ballplayer. (Mr. Brown, Mr. Brown...there is a place for you in baseball somewhere, maybe in Cooperstown, maybe in minor league bullpens, but somewhere.)

I remember reading an excerpt in *Harper's* about a Navajo's advice to white hunters: Start hunting two or three days before you go hunting. Look out your insurance agency window for deer. This is baseball.

In Oriental medicine, we say there are ten main meridians, or currents of life, or maybe it's eleven, or twelve, or fourteen, or twenty, or sometimes other numbers come into play. The trick is to get on the right one. Ballplayers are always trying to do this as well, to get in the flow, on the right meridian, and this is reflected in our pregame preparations and our superstitions and even our patterns of conversation, which is what got me started on this train of thought to begin with. When The Bear and Crandall were telling hunting stories, they weren't just hitting the highlights. They were trying to get the whole thing right. The dog didn't just get the bird. The dog had a certain pedigree and upbringing and overcame various obstacles and, as with children's stories and the Torah, certain anomalous moments have to be located just right. Then the dog gets the bird.

As I said, my interest would flag on that sort of thing, but that was okay because I was getting steadily more intoxicated, and sitting on my right were the Last Real Ballplayer and Paul "Wolfie"

Roberts. The Last Real Ballplayer was Rickie Stanton. Ricky was in his early 30's, a middle infielder who could play everywhere, even catch, in a pinch. He had a couple years in the big leagues, "about a hundred years", as he put it, in the minor leagues, and sometimes seemed to know everything that ever happened in baseball, and why. The Phillies had a rash of injuries mid-season and picked him up on waivers. As players got healthy, they sent him to Oklahoma City, perhaps to be called up at the end of the season, perhaps not.

Wolfie was about 35 and also had several years in the big leagues. He had played on a couple of the Orioles' World Series teams. Wolfie joined us in mid-season. He had been out of baseball for a year and a half, trying to dry out. It was a very unusual rehabilitation program at this point because his basic plan for staying off alcohol was to smoke enormous amounts of marijuana. That couldn't hold up under the stresses and temptations of a minor league season, so by this point Wolfie was way off the wagon. He and the Last Real Ballplayer were rooming together, a real quinella for you, as we used to say.

So I could hang out on the outskirts of The Bear's conversation, or I could swing around and watch Wolfie or listen to Ricky. Wolfie was a spectacle in himself, one moment trying out a few arthritic steps on the edge of the dance floor, the next moment leaning his long body over the counter of the bar to let a frightened bartender in on some secret, then disappearing altogether for a while, probably to step outside and howl at the moon.

One of the moments when Wolfie was gone, I swung around to see Ricky talking, or trying to talk, to what looked like a serious contender for the "Drunkest Woman on the Planet" award for that night. If Ricky was trying to get to first base with her, it seemed very clear she was having a hard time just getting the uniform on and making it out to the playing field.

Ricky: "So hello there. And what might your name be?"

Woman: Blank stare, but at least in Ricky's general direction.

Ricky: "Well as I said, my name's Rick and I'm a ballplayer. Do you like baseball?"

And so on. It was ridiculous. Finally we learned her name was Donna. She perked up considerably a few minutes later, though, after doing a couple lines of coke on the bar. I had never seen anyone do that before.

For the next hour or so, I rotated my attention between Rob and The Bear and watching Wolfie and listening to Ricky and Donna and admiring the old revolving Canadian Club sign with that very friendly-looking beautiful woman on one side and little balls of light bouncing off into the distance on the other. Also, sometime in there a snazzy-looking couple got on the dance floor (heretofore Wolfie's domain) and performed a half-hour or so of disco dancing. I had never seen that before either, and I marveled at it—how long did it take to learn those intricate maneuvers?

Once when I checked in on Ricky and Donna, it looked like her boyfriend had showed up. Whoever it was, she had unbuttoned his shirt and was sucking one of his nipples while rubbing his crotch. This didn't hurt seem to Ricky's feelings at all. The next time I looked over the mysterious stranger was gone and Ricky was buying her another drink.

At two in the morning, Rob and The Bear and I staggered back to the hotel. I don't know if you know minor league schedules. On a typical night, two is bad enough: you get out of the clubhouse between ten and eleven and go from there. But on an off-day, you have been up late the night before celebrating. The wakeup call is 6 a.m. You get to the Omaha airport at 7:15, way too early, for an 8:30 flight. (Only because it's an off-day, you don't bristle when a waitress asks, "So, any chance you guys'll ever make the pros?") An hour and a half in St. Louis, where you have the airport hot dogs for lunch. Braniff is notoriously late. You hit New Orleans by 2:30, check in at the hotel by 4:00. Then the drinking begins. I think professional football and basketball players are generally considered to be better natural athletes than baseball players. I know they look more impressive and imposing. At 5'10" and 165 pounds, the Last Real Ballplayer could have played in the same backfield with the Four Horseman of Notre Dame. But, as he used to say in our defense, "If you are not a world-class athlete in excellent physical condition, an off-day in the minor leagues can kill you." So, to make a long story short, when I say we staggered back to the hotel, I really mean it.

I drank a lot of beer in those days, but already could tell that tomorrow was going to be very unpleasant. About the only comfort I could find in situations like that was checking to see if other guys felt worse, which I did the next morning. I saw Rob first, in the lobby.

"Yo, Robbie, how you doing?"

"Well, first I woke up about ten and called Angie. Then I walked into the bathroom and called Ralph."

That made me feel a little better. Rob was a born-again Christian and rarely went in for the kind of drinking we had done the night before. I had to give him credit, though. When he went for it, he generally went all the way, and managed not to feel guilty about it until at least the next day. That's probably why he had called his wife the next morning. I don't know if the wives ever tuned into it, but I always thought that guilt accounted for a pretty large percentage of the morning phone calls when we were on road trips. It wasn't just sexual guilt. A guy might have had more to drink than his wife thinks he drinks. Or he might have said some stuff, usually pretty innocent stuff, to a barmaid. He might feel he fell off the marriage meridian, which is part of his pregame preparation, and feel a need to get back on before the next game. Of course, there were a lot of incoming morning phone calls on those road trips and, come to think of it, I'm not sure the guys ever tuned in to the idea that guilt could be behind those as well. Also, I'm not sure the wives had meridian theory, so maybe their guilt was just sexual.

Certainly one of the unique features of twentieth century existence involves hotel roommates, telephones, and conversations with loved ones. When else in human history have people talked privately with their husbands or wives while a friend or acquaintance lay in the bed next to them, listening, waiting patiently to go to dinner? Ballplayers don't have the usual anxieties. They don't care too much what the eavesdropper thinks of them. They're not all that worried about what is happening at home, barring some major problem. The important thing is to get the marriage meridian right. Maybe to say, at just the right time, what you said the last time you got three hits. Or, for the more evolved, simply to create the right feel. Hang up on the right note. That's the main thing.

To get back to Rob, he looked like hell but didn't seem to be too worried about it.

Then I bumped into Ricky. I made some joke about his efforts to talk to Donna. I really hadn't understood the whole thing to begin with. I guess I just thought he was drunk and bored, so it was an eye-opener of sorts when he said, "Oh, yeah, she was perfect. I thought I could get her drunk enough to come back to the room and we could all fuck her."

I'm no saint and I don't think I'm particularly naïve about sex, but I'd had no idea that was the plan. I changed the subject, "How's Wolfie doing?"

"His old lady called about nine this morning. After a couple minutes of minutes, he said, 'I've got to go to the bathroom, but don't hang up.' Forty minutes later he came back and she was still on the line. I guess you have to be an unusual sort of woman to hook up with Wolfie in the first place."

I think it was this that was so strange and even disturbing about Wolfie. It certainly wasn't the alcoholism, or that he was already hard at work destroying his third marriage, or that he had given his winter address on the team's Christmas card list as 68 El Camino, Anywhere, USA. It was that he had fallen so far off the baseball meridians, lost all care and respect for the gods.

We got on the bus about four that afternoon to ride to the ballpark, and I still wasn't feeling too frisky. We played these games in New Orleans at the Superdome. They were trying to attract a major league team then and had a Triple A team play a season there to demonstrate "viability". This was a joke. Minor league revenues probably couldn't pay the electric bill, but it was a fun place to play. This was my first game there. From a distance it looked like somebody had dropped a nuclear power plant with weird accessories into downtown New Orleans. Up close it looked more like a concrete-colored ladybug, giving the rest of the city a certain ominous air, as if downtown New Orleans were actually a collection of multi-eyed insects getting ready to jump into action. Part of this first impression could have been my hangover.

I was sitting at my locker a few minutes later when somebody dropped off the stat sheets. Usually before the first game of a series they would pass around a program insert that had the individual statistics of players on both teams. I had an intricate set of taboos that would determine each time whether or not I would look at the stats. I thought I knew what my average was but still—to actually look at it could be bad luck. But this was the last three games of the season, the die was pretty much cast, and I knew I was hitting slightly over .300.

They had it all wrong. Somehow I had lost two or three hits and my average was .292. It may not sound like much, but this was the minor leagues and if you lose two or three hits, even unofficially, it's not like anybody but you gives enough of a goddam about it to get it straightened out, which means it may never get straightened out. It's the worst luck of all to worry about your average, or complain about it, but this annoyed the hell out of me. I had sort of planned to skate through these last days, enjoy the end of a good season, and do whatever it took to stay above .300. But this felt entirely different. I know numbers don't lie, but it feels a hell of a lot easier to stay above .300 than to get above .300.

What is that old saying about when you need help the most, help will find you and often it comes from a most unexpected source? There I was sitting in front of my locker feeling hungover and sorry for myself when Robbie came over and sat down next to me.

"Want a little help for the game tonight?"

"I don't want a little help. I want a lot of help."

"How about a greenie?"

Well, yeah, how about a greenie. I had heard of "greenies," of course. It is the name players give to the amphetamines they take to improve their performance. You hear about them in the minor leagues, but I had never used any before or really known what they were or how to get them.

"You use those?"

"Yeah. They're great. You wanna try one or what?"

I didn't look at this as a temptation or a moral choice. I had no particular qualms about taking greenies. It simply never came up before. I didn't even find it particularly ironic that a born-again Christian was offering me my first one. In fact, I found that to be somewhat reassuring. The bottom line is that if you are hungover and playing your first ballgame in the Superdome and they have just lopped ten points off your average and a good Christian boy offers you something that might help, if you are me you grab the pill and hunt yourself up a glass of water, which is what I did.

There is a routine for taking greenies. You get used to the effects and they are completely predictable for the most part, so that your pregame preparation becomes an interesting and occasionally intricate countdown to blastoff. Sometime I will describe that routine. It was an enjoyable one to go through, so I will probably enjoy describing it. But, as this was my first time, I don't remember any of that.

All I know is this was one of the most fun games I ever played. I think I would have enjoyed it whether I played well or not, but as it turned out I went four for five with two doubles (so I could say to hell with the crummy statisticians) and just generally felt quite happy to be spending my mortal life playing ball there in the Superdome. I never knew there were so many pleasant things to think about in between pitches when you are playing right field.

The first time up I singled to center. I ran to first base about a hundred miles an hour and made a wide turn. Second base had never looked so close and for a moment I thought I could turn a routine single into a double. Of course I had no chance and I retreated safely back to first. That was my only brush with aberrant behavior. Otherwise I was pretty much just focused and happy.

Some of the guys on the team knew what I was doing and that I was doing it for the first time, and every once in a while they would nudge each other and smile in my direction. Of course I would just smile right back at them. I was having a hell of a time.

We got absolutely slaughtered that night and Wolfie came in to pitch the bottom of the eighth, when the game was well out of reach. He was probably still legally drunk, but he got them out in order. He might have been our only pitcher to do that all night. With two outs and two strikes on the last batter, he turned to our shortstop and said in a voice they probably heard down on Bourbon Street, "Watch this yakker."

Then he turned and threw a tremendous overhand curveball which the batter took for strike three. As he walked off the field, Wolfie gestured to the crowd (all five hundred of them) and the rest of us wildly, as if he had done something great, which in a way he had. But in the larger context of this hopelessly lost game, at the tail end of another minor league season, it seemed a little bizarre.

The locker room, despite the loss, was a pretty pleasant place. Two more games to go and two more nights in New Orleans. Wolfie tried to console the younger pitchers who had been shelled that night. At one point he said, “Hell, it’s easier pitching in the big leagues than it is down here. In the big leagues, you just gotta figure how many milligrams they’re taking and pitch ‘em accordingly. Here, you don’t know what the hell they’re doing.”

I had to admit it was an analysis that made perfect sense to me.

## Amphetamine Story No. 2

Lately I have been thinking about what it will actually be like to conduct classes, what kind of atmosphere do I want to have (or will I have, whether I want it or not) and the goofiest image keeps popping up. This is a long story and it starts with, of all people, Bob Uecker. Uecker was the Brewers radio announcer when I was with them and he was a genuinely, incredibly funny guy. We'd take a bus from the airport to the hotel and he'd get on the microphone and do a thirty-minute monologue that made me marvel (and laugh)—much wittier than his public personality as a dumb fan or Mr. Baseball.

When Uecker was still a player he was traded from the Phillies to the Braves. This was when the Phillies had a legendary brand of clubhouse amphetamine called "Red Juice." It was passed around openly by the trainers and must have really been something because ten years after it was officially dropped, or banned, you would still hear Red Juice stories.

Anyway, Uecker took some with him when he went over to the Braves. He joined them for a day game after the Braves had played the night before and was sitting around the clubhouse on that first day when Clete Boyer came in and walked directly to the nearest trash can and threw up. Everything in his demeanor made it clear this wasn't a case of the stomach flu. Uecker took Boyer aside and gave him some Red Juice and forgot about it.

Pitchers and reserves hit fungoes during infield practice (I think every child who goes to a big league game early remembers that routine), so Uecker was out on the field before it started. This was one of those parks where the ballplayers emerge from a tunnel in the outfield. Everyone was getting ready for infield—a dry routine but part of the work—when all of a sudden there's a loud, long Tarzan yell coming from the mouth of the tunnel. It's Boyer, of course, and he sprints full speed from the outfield to his third base position where he launches into a headfirst slide into the bag, jumps to his feet, and gives everyone a huge grin. Not a typical approach to taking infield.

I've never forgotten that story. Partly, of course, it is about drugs, and if it's wrong to find humor or feel anything about taking drugs besides just saying no, then I'm a bad guy. But primarily it's about waking up out of the humdrum and anxiety and not living in the here and now (whatever it may have taken to accomplish that) to feel the incredible power and joy and smiles of being alive. If you're just alive to play third base today, then play the shit out of it.

It also reminds me of a famous acupuncture treatment by some old master. A patient's progress wasn't going well (in the case of master practitioners, this is more the patient's fault than the practitioner's), so the acupuncturist waited behind his door and struck the patient hard on the head with a martial arts stick as he walked in for treatment. It changed everything, partly because of the exact acupuncture point on the top of the head.

What does all this have to do with teaching, you might ask? I have no idea, but I can't escape the image of myself beginning a class (don't worry, not the first day) with a huge yell from the doorway followed by a sprint across the room and ending with a magnificent slide into the cabinets. It is very important to get up and share the resulting grin. This is not showing off, but trying to give something.

This is supposed to be funny—I'm smiling as I write this and I smile every time I think of the Clete Boyer story. But I'm sure there's a reason I've been thinking this way. This general sense in education of frustration, anxiety, time-on-task, responsibility, desire for results and validation—the idea of school as a place where teachers sit and hear each other groan, this mentality I feel in my observation experience and which seems to be the underpinning of the professional education, like the latest theory is a light that can lift us out of this scary darkness—all this I am going to counter with a simple, joyful, leg-breaking slide. And to hell with the strawberries.

## Mazatlan '74

We arrived in Mazatlan in midafternoon. The trip down had been fairly uneventful, aside from the van breaking down in Del Rio and my poor navigational skills resulting in our going several hundred miles out of the way. To make up lost time, I decided to cross the border at Agua Prieta instead of Nogales—several Mexican friends commenting later: "You came down through Cananea? That road is dangerous."

And yet what I remember most is simply driving south at night through the Sonoran Desert on old Highway 15 (it was still two lanes then) and seeing small fires burning off in the distance. You couldn't see the people you knew had to be sitting beside them, warming themselves, which made it impossible, for me at least, not to think about them, wish to join them, wonder what, if any, connection I had with them, here or in eternity. In 1974, the way the world was then, the way I was then, those fires were somehow the most inviting and yet also the loneliest things I ever saw in my life.

This was the first week Patti and I lived together. To begin our lives together by heading out to Mexico in her Ford van with her big Great Dane in the back, along with most of what we owned, was pretty exciting. Now, almost thirty years later, after all the strange and wonderful and life-draining things that have happened to us, I know there are times our kids haven't the slightest idea what holds us together. They don't know we were once young and in love and driving across the continent with absolutely no clue about what we were doing. It's a very deep bond.

We went first in Mazatlan to the Hotel Decima, which is on the tourist strip by the beach, just down from Senor Frog's, because I had been told that was where the American players were staying.

At the front desk I learned the only ballplayer staying there was Jack Pierce. I went up to his room and knocked on the door.

Jack was large and reasonably friendly. He moved around the room with the kind of grace certain large people have—like Babe Ruth or Jackie Gleason.

We checked each other out.

Jack: "So where'd you play last year?"

"Just half a year in Rookie League and then the Instructional League."

"They sent you down here with just that?"

"Yeah, how about you?"

"I was with Louisville last summer—the Braves Triple A team. They called me up for the last month of the season."

"To Atlanta?"

"Yeah."

If he was trying to impress me, he had. Then he asked what position I played and when I said: "first base," I saw that momentary frozen look of concern—the Wally Pip look—I was to get to know so well and which probably graced my own face more than once. You don't have to be in the big leagues to feel it. You can be in Double A, having an okay year, planning to move upward and onward when you hear about a new kid tearing them up in A ball. All of a sudden you're not on the way up, you're on the way out. I think everybody feels it, from established stars to the lowliest minor leaguers. Most stars, in my opinion, pretended to ignore it, but not all of them. One spring the Phillies had a young pitcher named Steve Waterbury who manager Danny Ozark clearly liked and seemed to be trying to find a spot for. There wasn't one. The bullpen was set with fixtures like Ron Reed and Tug McGraw. But one morning Reed was warming up on the side and Waterbury got a little too close to his catcher—maybe ten feet off to the side—and Reed buzzed him about ninety miles an hour very close to his head. I always thought it was a Wally Pipp thing.

Pete Rose dealt with it in the cleanest, most straightforward way I ever saw, as he did with just about everything else about baseball when I was around him. When he came to the Phillies in '79, I was the backup first baseman behind him in spring training. The interest in the Phillies and Pete Rose joining the team was tremendous then. Reporters chronicled his every move. On top of that he got off to a terrible start in spring training games. I filled in for him in late innings and had a great spring— couple of pinch-hit home runs, etc. Everybody knew it meant nothing. Maybe I could make the team in a backup role if I kept playing well (I did keep playing well; I didn't make the team.) But still, the Wally Pipp thing. One day I ripped a double off the right field wall. When I came back to the dugout, Pete picked up his stuff, walked toward the clubhouse, and said jokingly: "Man, you're going to drive me to the American League." That, I always thought, was very good, making a joke that both conveyed respect and dealt openly with the Wally Pipp demon.

Jack's first comment, when I said I played first base, was: "Well, I play first base here."

"Oh. Well, I also play the outfield."

"Yeah. Maybe they got you to play right field. Adolfo hasn't hit shit this month and I heard they're paying him a lot of money."

After this exchange, which was a little sobering, I learned the married players were staying at apartments a mile or two down the beach. It was growing dark as we headed down to find either an apartment or some other Americans. It was one of those moments we were wondering just what the hell we were doing, and why.

We couldn't find the apartments we were looking for but we did finally see a sign on what looked like a very large house that said, in English: "Apartment for rent."

It was perfect: A large one-bedroom apartment across the street from the beach for $200 a month. Beautiful tile floors and a patio in the back that overlooked a veranda. We moved our stuff in—it took about ten minutes—and sat on the couch together and felt like different people than the ones we had been half an hour ago. They didn't mind about Sadye, the Great Dane. They didn't care that we weren't married. In a bizarre burst of Midwestern guilt, I had felt compelled to tell them that, a kind of candor that I think was very puzzling to our Mexican landlords.

About seven o'clock it seemed clear we should get over to the ballpark and find out what I had got myself into.

We arrived at the stadium just about at game time. It seemed strange to be pulling up to a ballpark with the lights on and the stadium full. I found my way to the general manager's office, got all the introductions and the contract signing over with, then made my way down to the dugout and locker room, where they had a uniform for me that fit.

There were five or six other Americans on the team. Three were pitchers: Randy Boyd, Joe "The Animal" Pactwa, and Don Criekey. The left fielder was Charley Howard, who had just finished his fifteenth year in the minor leagues, all in the Pirates organization, without ever playing a day in the big leagues.

Everybody was reasonably friendly to me, especially the pitchers after they learned I was an everyday player.

There is, or there used to be, a conventional wisdom that native Mexican ballplayers are not quite as good as their counterparts in Puerto Rico, the Dominican Republic, and Venezuela, but our team had several fine players. Hector Torres, who played for about ten years in the big leagues, was our playing manager. Carlos Lopez was our center fielder. He also made it to "The Show" for a few seasons. And Aurelio Lopez, who pitched for years with the Tigers, was our bullpen stopper.

The "Adolfo" that Jack Pierce referred to turned out to be Adolfo Phillips. This was a major shock. As a child, I had been a serious baseball fan and he had been one of my favorite players—a center fielder for the Cubs. He played in the major leagues for many years, making, I think, an All-Star team or two.

Adolfo Adolfo Adolfo—didn't you save any of that money you made? His last season in the big leagues had been a year or two before. Where he had been playing since, and how he had wound up here, I couldn't have imagined.

He seemed to go out of his way to be friendly to me that night. Under only slightly different circumstances, I would have asked for his autograph. I was mindful enough of what Jack had said, though, to note that he went 0-4.

I still remember him sitting on the top step of the dugout during our half innings at bat, playing with pieces of dirt or picking aimlessly at a large callous on his thumb. You can tell a lot about players by the way they sit in the dugout. Some guys are very neat. They sit in the same spot for most of the game and keep their whole area clear of jackets and sunflower seeds and tobacco juice. Some guys, like Adolfo on that night, seem to be attracted to sitting on concrete steps and playing in the dirt. It's an awkward pose, one leg over the other and your butt half off the step. It reminded me a little of housewives in bathrobes, smoking cigarettes and letting themselves go. When I think of Jesus drawing in the dirt before saying: "Let him who is without guilt..." I think of ballplayers and dugout steps.

Ralph Houk used to manage from that spot until one night in New York he was playing around in the dirt when a large bolt landed with incredible force about six inches from his hand. Someone apparently found it in the stands and just let it fly, probably from the top tier of the stadium. If it had hit him in the head, he would have been killed. I think the rest of his career, at least when he was in New York, he managed from the bench.

Just sitting on the bench for that first game was a powerful experience. The night air was cool but dry. I found myself wondering: it's still baseball, half these guys are American, what is it that's so different? Of course it was a lot of things—the smells, the language of the fans, the half-strange, half-familiar introductions coming over the loudspeakers, and the mariachi band behind home plate.

In the U.S. the lines between players and fans and the playing field are clearly drawn. We love these distinctions. In Mexico all that begins to break down. The fields are not in such great shape; uniforms are sometimes dirty and some players are at the pinnacle of success while others are young Mexican kids who have never been out of their hometowns before.

Late in the game it got cool and the fans built several fires in the stands down each foul line.

We were playing Guaymas that night. Maury Wills was their manager. His son Bump had just got out of college and was playing shortstop for them. In the top of the seventh, behind by two runs, Wills made Hector Espino lay down a sacrifice bunt. Hector Espino is the Babe Ruth of Mexican baseball. A fan yelled down: “Wills, por que?” It seemed like a pretty good question.

When you play in Mexico, you almost always wear your uniform to the park and shower afterward at your home or in your motel room. After the game, which we wound up losing 5-3 (Hector Espino hit a grand slam in the top of the ninth), we all filed out into the parking lot with the rest of the fans to go home. I found Patti at the box office gate, and we walked through the dwindling crowd together. From a distance we heard Sadye barking. We broke into a trot as we realized she was really frantic. As we got closer to the van, we could see a crowd gathering around and could hear people yelling and swearing, in both Spanish and English. We could see Sadye with her nose pressed up against the windshield, barking for all she was worth. We always worried about the dog getting into trouble in Mexico.

What was really going on was incredibly strange and surprising.

Mexican kids are always asking for baseballs, "pelotas," when they are around ballplayers. You get the idea it's not for a souvenir but just to have one to play with because balls are really that scarce. Apparently a twelve or thirteen-year-old kid had asked Joe Pactwa repeatedly for a ball. Joe said no several times and the kid cursed him in Spanish. Joe had been playing in Mexico long enough to understand exactly what he said, not that this should have mattered. He completely lost his temper, grabbing the kid and smashing him up against the first available car he found, which happened to be our van. He yelled at him and slapped him around while Sadye went crazy.

You can imagine how Mexican fans reacted to this. I had visions of a riot, which was overly dramatic. They probably would have just kicked the shit out of Joe and maybe the two or three other American males who were standing around. Fortunately, Hector Torres was nearby and stepped in and defused the situation. He probably saved both the kid and Joe.

The crowd broke up and seemingly all was forgotten quickly. I heard one fan say, in English, as he walked away: "You are an animal."

Patti and I laughed about it later that night, but not until we were well into our second six-pack of Carta Blanca. I had never known that kind of fear. As it unfolded, almost cinematically, first I was afraid for the dog, then for the kid, then for Joe, and then for myself, all in rapid succession.

The next morning I went to the ball park to pick up travel money. I learned that Adolfo Phillips had been released. I never saw or heard of him again.

## Please Release Me

I want to write here about being released, which is baseball terminology for getting fired. Playing in the minor leagues can be a surreal experience, primarily because the big leagues can seem like a distant pipe dream unless and until you actually get there. But there is some concreteness to it. The fundamental defining reality, of course, is: Do you find yourself in "The Show" or don't you? Along the way, the basic question is: Are you a prospect or a suspect? But almost everyone can kid themselves about that, and they are nebulous labels anyhow, so that for many players, the crucial reality sandwich is the day they are released. It is not necessarily final. Sometimes players who are released sign with other organizations and make it to the big leagues, but this is relatively rare, and I think it's safe to say that at the time you get your papers, it feels very final.

The threat of being released casts a huge shadow over the minor leagues. It can happen at any time. Players are released over the winter, during spring training (especially), and during the season. The largest percentage of players are released at the time it would seem to be most cruel: at the very end of spring training as teams reach their final shape. It's cruel because a player has gone through a whole winter and spring preparing himself to play a regular season and at the moment the bell is ringing for everyone else, it tolls for him.

Players have a lot of denial about their prospects for being released. This is understandable in lots of ways. First of all, to dwell on it too much will affect your game. But also you must realize that these are guys who have been elite athletes all their lives. Being cut is something that happens to someone else. This is not just their hope; it has been their experience all their lives.

Spring training is a very difficult time. There are two factors at work for many players. One is that they may have to play well in spring training games even to be considered for making a team. The other is that, even if they play well, they may get crunched by the numbers. It works this way: forty or fifty players start out on the major league team. Only twenty-five make the final roster. The rest are released or sent down to one of the minor league teams. An organization's minor league spring training camp (held in a different location) starts out with more than full rosters for each level of play (the Triple A team, Double A team, etc.). As the players start coming down from the big league team, there is a ripple effect throughout the organization. Players at each level are either released or sent down a notch. In other words, there's virtually no place to go except down or out.

So players at the end of spring training are trying to get their game faces on, trying to figure out how they are going to get their wives and families to Reading or Oklahoma City or Rocky Mount, and then often are called into the office on literally the last day of spring training and given their release.

As I said, there is a lot of denial by players about their own likelihood of being released, but from the outside (that is, players who are relatively safe for that year—the prospects), it can be fairly obvious. I always thought this metaphor was appropriate: A long time ago, I saw a Jacques Cousteau special where one fish out of a large school was trapped by some fish-eating plant. A diver intervened and released the fish, which appeared to be unharmed but in a bit of a daze. In about two seconds, a large predator fish arrived seemingly from nowhere and snatched the fish that had been released from the plant. A guy on the verge of being released is often like that fish. He's still on the bus, but there's something different about him.

Although we seldom talked openly about being released, I do remember one outlet for expression. In the late 60's there was a corny Englebert Humperdinck hit called "Please Release Me." These were the days when an average pop song still penetrated everyone's consciousness. Each interminable chorus began with the lines: "Please release me / Let me go." Probably once a week or so, in the clubhouse before or after a game, someone would launch into a half-comic, half-plaintive chorus of "Please Release Me." Often the singer would be a once-great prospect whose career was winding down. There were several sides to this. It was one part plea for euthanasia, one part an attempt to invoke the Reverse Athlete's Hex (by talking about it openly, I'll make it not happen), and one part a simple strategy for dealing with a bad game during a difficult season.

Let me illustrate all this with a story that, in a sense, covers almost my entire life of playing ball. I grew up in Findlay, Ohio. In my era, covering at least a couple decades, three players from my high school signed professional baseball contracts, and we all came pretty close together in time. One was me, of course. One was Mark Ammons, who was two years ahead of me in school. The third was Chuck Rogers, two years behind me, so that I played in high school with both of them.

We had what were probably the natural reversals of fortune in our respective amateur and professional careers. Far and away the best high school player was Chuck. As a pitcher, he led our team to the state tournament as a sophomore, then a state championship the next year, and a return to the finals when he was a senior. As a professional, he made it to the Triple A level with the Cubs, where he had several solid seasons, winning ten or eleven games a year, as I recall, for very mediocre teams. I played against him in the years I was with the Phillies' Triple A team in Oklahoma City. Remarkably, when we were kids in Little League, he played for the Lions' Cubs; I played for the National Lime and Stone Phillies.

Mark was the second best high school athlete, very good at both baseball and basketball. He played baseball in college just up the road in Bowling Green, where he was Mid-American Conference Player of the Year in 1973. As a professional with the Phillies, he played a year and a half of A ball before being released, than half a season as a player-coach with the Pirates' A team.

I did some good things in high school sports, but I didn't really grow up physically till after graduation so that I was much better comparatively as an adult, professional athlete than I had been as a teenager. I was more successful at the Triple A level than Chuck, for instance, and I was also the only one of us to make it, however briefly, to the big leagues.

This is mainly a story about Mark. He loved to play sports. He was one of Findlay's best athletes in Little League, Pony League, and high school. He didn't exactly come from "the wrong side of the tracks," but Findlay could be a pretty snobby little rich town (the home of Marathon Oil) where a lot of people tended to look down on residents of the lower-middle class neighborhood he lived in, the same neighborhood in which my wife grew up.

Mark had a distinctive personality. I liked him a lot. He was successful and competitive athletically but not macho or petty, which was unusual then and probably still is now. He had a way with teenage slang and could launch into a story and get so carried away with it that what came out was a series of rhythmic sentences, each one ending comically at a heightened pitch and volume, a kind of rising hysteria.

He didn't get a basketball scholarship out of high school, as other less deserving players from Findlay did, for reasons that were not very clear. I'd heard that the high school basketball coach refused to push any buttons for him, an explanation of events that rang very true for me when I first heard it. Our high school basketball coach was a very "political" animal. You had to know Findlay and Mark's neighborhood.

Mark played a Rookie League season in 1973 and at Spartanburg (low A) in 1974. He never did too well. He had to play either shortstop, where he wasn't that good defensively, or first base, which was essentially hopeless because he didn't hit for power.

I started with the Phillies in Rookie League in 1974 where I hit .344 with sixteen home runs in 58 games. I was invited to the Instructional League that fall, which sort of made me a prospect.

My wife and I have known each other since we were twelve or thirteen, but we didn't get involved romantically until that summer of '74. In the two or three weeks between the end of the regular season and the beginning of the Instructional League, I went back to Findlay and stayed with her in the small cottage she was renting. Mark was staying at his parents' home, two or three blocks away.

The local paper did an article on Mark and his career then. He was in a difficult position in describing his progress. They asked him about me, probably having no idea or concern where I was then. I had no family ties in Findlay at that point and had never been much of a local boy. Mark gave me a true left-handed compliment, saying the great thing I had going for me was that I was a left-handed hitter, which the organization needed badly. This was basically B.S., but I didn't mind, partly because I didn't know whether or not it was true.

The next morning Mark stopped in at Patti's house to apologize about the article. I didn't think he even knew I was in town. We hadn't met or talked in several years. He had his old sidekick, Dean Schrier, with him, whom I had known forever. The thing I remember is the way Mark was dressed. Disco was just coming in and at ten in the morning, in Findlay, Ohio, and for no apparent reason he looked, well, dandy. It was actually pretty cool.

As I said, Patti grew up in the same neighborhood as Mark. Mark was the local hero and a pretty good one at that, and when Patti was about twelve (Mark was two years older than both of us), Mark had been her "first kiss." She was thrilled, and then Mark tried to feel her up. Patti just walked away. When Mark sat in Patti's living room that morning in 1974, he described her this way: "Patti's got her own piece of mind." It was as neat a little summary as you could get of Patti and Findlay and Mark.

I went over to Mark's house a few days later for a party. Some of his friends were there, people I had always known, as well as his parents, and we all drank beer. Dean Schrier was there. Dean had been a marginal high school basketball player with one moment of glory: In a JV basketball game, with one second to go, he took an inbounds pass at half court and launched a perfect desperation shot which won the game by a point. From the vantage point of being three or four years younger, I saw Dean's whole career, from junior high through high school, including the summers in between at the Y gym, his future career as a manager of a local grocery store, and his marriage and divorce. He idolized Mark.

That night Dean got drunk and for some reason Mark had him strip down to his jockey shorts and, after an introduction mentioning in some way the Impossible Shot, made him dance to some popular record. It was funny and a little strange, but I always remembered the half-hysteria in Mark's voice encouraging Dean and Dean dancing nonstop until he wound up in the backyard throwing up.

Mark and I were in spring training together the next year. We didn't hang out together. I had bypassed him. I was working out with the Double A team. He was with the high A team.

He really didn't have a chance. He didn't have a position. He didn't hit for power. His best skills were mediocre for professional baseball. At some level, he knew it; he had his protective mechanisms up. He had described the experience of playing in the minor leagues as "a good summer job."

At the end of that spring training he was released. It was inevitable. And yet the night before he was to fly home, as I was coming down the motel steps to go to dinner (we all stayed at the same Days Inn), I heard his distinctive half-comic, half-hysterical chant coming from some motel room. He was with two or three other players, they had obviously been drinking, and he was letting everything out, reviewing, almost Homerically, the story of his career and what he had done well and what the players who were kept instead of him had done poorly and all in a voice that took me back to my childhood. I don't know if I can describe it. It starts softly, usually with "and," and ends loudly in a varying mixture of humor and sarcasm and incredulity and tears. The mixture depended on the situation. This time it was over the edge, closer to crying than anything else. The pacing was constant. Extra clauses got thrown in with great rapidity, like playing the old game with a marble, *Shoot the Moon*.

"And all I did in the one chance I got to play was go 13 for 28."

"And all Skalisky ever did was hit ten home runs for the whole season and never hit the cutoff man and tell all the coaches he could have played football for NOTRE DAME." And so on.

Mark is dead now, of colon cancer. It was diagnosed in 1978 and he died in 1981. I talked to him once in those years. He was doing pretty well at the time and sounded good. By all accounts, he handled it well. An old friend of mine saw him down at the Y once in 1980 cleaning out his gym basket (probably the same one he'd had since he was about ten). My friend thought he looked thin and asked how he was feeling. Mark said it looked like he was fading out.

Mark's best friend from baseball who made it in the big leagues was Randy Lerch, which was a little funny because Lerch and I never hit it off that well personally, and we were both with the Brewers in spring training in '81, when Mark died. Lerch had talked with him on the phone a few weeks earlier. I only remember a few snippets of the conversation. Mark said that he (Lerch) and Tug McGraw were the only players he respected and then that he had to go, before he started crying.

What I've always wondered is, did he ever let it out about dying in that wail and chant which is now more a part of me than it is of him? Do any of us? My wife and I both loved him and think of him often, and when I think of what I know about how joy and pain and humor and death can be caught in a human voice, I think about Mark and my wife and Findlay, Ohio and Dean Schrier and even Randy Lerch, and I see myself standing transfixed on a stairwell in Clearwater, Florida, listening maybe to human history and my personal history coming together like a thunderclap.

## Baseball Enlightenment

When you are 26 years old and have zero hits
          in your 5 pinch-hits appearances in the
               Major Leagues
          and you are playing for the Phillies in '79
               when they drew
          over 30,00 for every home game despite
               finishing fourth
                    in the division
and Dickie Noles has just pitched 9 beautiful shut
   out innings
          and you are sent up to pinch-hit for him
             with two outs
               in the bottom of the ninth and the
                    score tied 0-0 and
                              the bases are empty
and Bruce Sutter is pitching for the Cubs and this
   was one
          of those years he was virtually unhittable
and you think there may be something funny about
   this business
          of playing in the Big Leagues but you can't
               quite put
                    your finger on it

maybe it's the Astroturf,
maybe it's the ghost of
Josh Gibson, maybe it's just
you, or maybe it's
something else altogether—
and presumably the one thing you can do
now that will make
everything clear is hit a home run but
what, really, are the odds?
And as your name is announced over the loud-
speakers, amidst
these 30,00 people, the only sound you
hear is the beer vendors
hawking their wares—that
old shuffle and cry:
that is the sound of one
hand clapping

## Casey Revisited: The Culture of Baseball

Although I spent a good portion of my first thirty years on this planet playing baseball, it is only recently, years after I walked off my last ball field, that I asked myself for the first time: what is a ball? Specifically, what is a ball in sports? Usually when I think of some basic question like this, I can go back to my childhood and remember some initial hit or impression I may have completely forgotten, but this time I drew a blank.

I've thought about it a lot since and have come to believe that for all the gibberish aficionados of one sport or another put out about why their particular favorites are distinctive, or special, the bottom-line distinction baseball can claim is that the ball serves a fundamentally different purpose than in most, if not all, other sports.

Let me put it this way: in other sports such as football or basketball, the ball is simply a physical representation of the participants' egos. Or one could call it a trophy, an icon, etc. The games are symbolic warfare—rather than killing the enemy, you overwhelm him and plant your flag, or your scent, or your trophy, or your ego in his end zone or goal. I imagine ancient games arising from a high priest tossing out a ball which represents divine favor or something like that. I would guess it only represented the high priest's ego, making that high priest the spiritual forebear of modern-day team owners.

The analogy doesn't work so well for baseball because somewhere along the line some genius came up with the idea of a bat. Maybe the original impetus for baseball was symbolic warfare and maybe the bat and ball are symbolic weapons (I would question even that—you simply can't simulate baseball with clubs and rocks), but then at some point the bat and ball stopped being weapons and started being tools and we literally and very basically have baseball as a "skill" sport. Certainly other sports require skills or techniques but not in my opinion the same way baseball does.

So the ball is not a trophy but a tool. (Pitchers describe hitting the corners as "painting the black.") The bat is also not a weapon but a tool. Enormous contrasts with other sports arise from this. Teams in other sports are little armies. They have the specialization of activity, group strategies, and so on that armies employ to win wars. Baseball teams are guilds. Varied specialists do their work with a fair degree of independence and combine with others to fashion a product—which happens to be victory in a ball game. Incidentally, I don't think it's a coincidence the Baseball Players Association has been far and away the most effective and cohesive union in sports. Certainly there are specific historical circumstances involved such as the baseball players having Marvin Miller, who was brilliant, on their side, but the simple fact is that baseball players are craftsman who tend to have a union mentality while football players, for instance, are warriors—not so apt to have the right spirit for collective bargaining.

This accounts for one of my favorite characteristics about baseball—it actively discourages the macho spirit of triumph that other sports actively encourage. There is a primitive male dominance at the bottom of these other sports. Certainly it's better to dunk a basketball over an opponent or score a touchdown against him that it is to kill him and steal his women, but the spirit to me is the same so these other sports lend themselves to display, braggadocio, and so on.

Again the important thing is not just that the ball is a tool but that the bat is a second, different tool. The skills of pitching and hitting are totally unrelated. When you are successful in baseball you don't feel so much that you've beaten the other person as that you've finished a job. The macho thing crops up in baseball because it's powerfully in our culture, maybe in our male genes, but it feels comical and inappropriate when it arises. For example, when a powerfully-built home run hitter strikes out against a junkball pitcher (slow curve in the dirt) or feebly grounds out back to the mound (a special humiliation) the frustration can sometimes be too much and he'll yell from the dugout, "Throw that shit over the plate." In other words, come out and fight like a man. This gives everybody a good laugh, most especially the pitcher. Even the home run hitter, if he's good, will usually laugh about it later. It's funny because it's just not that kind of a battle.

The ongoing tension and dynamic cooperation between hitter and pitcher contribute to this. No pitcher strikes everybody out. No hitter is impossible to strike out. It's more like the continuous struggles in nature—the balance between predator and prey, for instance, with constant adaptations and interdependence—than in other sports where defeat is a symbolic death.

I want to elaborate on this idea that pitchers and hitters use different skills insofar as this contrasts with most other sports. In football and basketball the physical attributes required to play offense and defense are essentially the same. Matchups are based on size and strategy but it boils down basically to my speed and strength against yours. Victories are personal. Baseball is once removed from that and this distinction is vital. In short, your skill defeated mine today. Mine may win tomorrow. I can live with that.

The clearest example I can give of all this is the Dodgers-A's World Series a few years ago. The A's were supposed to be invincible and their physically imposing home run hitters had adopted the macho forearm bash as a ritual display after hitting home runs. To me this behavior is a kind of pollutant from other sports. What do you the next time you strike out—commit suicide?

At any rate, the Dodgers had the superior pitching skill and won easily, but the key moment for me was when Mickey Hatcher, a nerdy-looking reserve, hit a home run, walked through the dugout after circling the bases and did a mock forearm bash with a wimpy-looking trainer, after which both recoiled in feigned agony. That sums up the macho side of baseball for me: Humor pops it like a balloon.

All of this may or may not be complete nonsense but it is at least the basis for what I would offer as a new reading of "Casey at the Bat". For me, "Casey" is one of those myths that derives its power from the strangeness and mystery of the tale. Something is askew, but what? If it came down to us in stone tablets, we would suspect something is missing, or the translation is obscure.

The "mystery" is that baseball is different than other sports. Casey is a war hero. That model works well in other sports where the simple physical attributes are so crucial to success.

People bring these expectations to baseball, where they don't work. Here's the real story of the Casey myth: He was an imposing-looking player with limited skill. Every once in a while he hit the longest home runs in recent memory. He was only the Dave Kingman of small-town America local teams, but because they didn't understand baseball so well, he was viewed as a kind of good-guy Goliath. Nobody cared he only hit .210 every year; they just wanted to talk about the mammoth home runs. Casey played into this adulation in the best possible way—he accepted it silently with a false modesty. What else could he do? The truth is he wasn't all that good, but who can say that about themselves? To embellish on his home runs would make somebody inevitably ask—Why don't you do it more often? Very important for that question to go unasked.

The real hero was the pitcher on the other team, but he didn't look or act like a hero. He was small, unprepossessing, and didn't talk much about pitching, not because of false modesty but because he didn't want to give away his secrets while he was still playing. He had a great curve and could throw it on three and two. Casey could hit a belt-high fastball a million miles but he was helpless against the pitcher who could throw his fastball where he wanted to and his curve for strikes.

In some earlier game, in late innings and with a comfortable lead, our pitcher had grooved a 2-0 fastball to Casey and given up a legendary home run. The locals felt sorry for the pitcher but there was a method in this madness. He knew Casey would look for that pitch again forever.

So the stage is set for the big game and the dramatic showdown. Casey is looking for the fastball he can kill because he got it before and because it's all he can hit and he doesn't know anything about pitching. Our pitcher starts him off with two hellacious curve balls (we used to call them "bowel-lockers"). Casey doesn't swing because he's completely dumfounded by them, but he has to play the part he's created for himself, so he quiets down the crowd. The pitcher can do about anything he wants with Casey at this point, but on the off chance Casey learned from the other two curves, he wastes a fastball up and in, maybe six inches out of any zone Casey can reach. Casey is so excited to see a fastball he unleashes a tremendous swing. Who can tell besides the pitcher that he missed by a foot, that it was never in doubt? This *is* the stuff legends are made of, but we got the wrong guy. We've got to dump Casey and revive the memory of that long-lost pitcher. Then we'll start to understand baseball.

*26 December 2006*

## Acid Droppers and Fly Catchers

Dear Mr. Poff,

I am working with my son on a mammoth project of asking each and every player who has ever been in the majors to tell what his greatest thrill-most memorable moment was. We would like to publish all these responses so that your memories, insights and feelings are forever remembered. My sincerest thanks and I have enclosed a stamped return envelope. Take care.

*Sincerely,*

Okay

It was in the summer of '78
I was playing in Oklahoma City,
The old American Association,
With teams in cities like Des Moines and
    Denver,
Omaha and Indianapolis.

The 89'ers were still playing at
The fairgrounds stadium, just west of
    downtown,
Where the wind blew out to left nearly
Every night—a hard, hot wind coming up
From Texas with the smell of Cadillacs and
Easy money (that part of the country
Was booming in the 70's) and summer's
    vast expanse.
One of the most certain things in my life
    then
Was to pull into the players' parking lot
And see the flag extended straight, always
In the same direction—like the flag in
The shot of the astronauts on the moon.
It was a paradise for right-handed hitters,
Or supposed to be, although some lost
Their stroke trying to lift and pull the ball
All the time and correspondingly some
    left-handers
(Dane Iorg for example), faced with a right
    field fence
You couldn't reach on most nights with a
    cannon,
Actually learned how to hit there.

The story at hand is this:

There was a group of us back in those
  days,
Solid professional baseball players,
Most with some time in the big leagues
Who were now growing old in the minors,
Who still had some roots in the good old
  60's,
And who probably, to be a little honest,
Wanted to outdo the brothers on the team
(By that I mean those brothers who
  smoked pot
During the day and wore sunglasses
  everywhere
And went to the ballpark at night and
  kicked ass)
And so we formed the 1st unofficial
"Acid Droppers and Fly Catchers Club"—
  the idea
Being we would drop acid and play a
Triple A ballgame successfully—with
No discernible lapse in our, honestly,
High standard of baseball professionalism
(Not exactly "grace under pressure,"
  perhaps,
But maybe you can get the concept)

The time for me to launch came on a fine
    sunny
Saturday in July—a day game—as
Rare in the minors as a fat postman.
This was when I was reading Lao-Tzu
And thinking continually of dualism
And the Big Bang and time and space
(I can prove this: the summer before,
    in Reading, I wrote this poem between
    pitches one night in left field

*Beauty of stillness*
*10 million earth rivers*
        *empty into ocean*
*Night into day*
*Life into death*

    Yeah!)

And especially I remembered reading
About *yin and yang*—the expression was
    not
Part of our culture then—how the original
Chinese characters for this idea which
Seems to sum up the truth of the whole
    universe
Simply stood for

“the sunny side of the hill” and
“the shady side of the hill”

So there I was, pre-game, officially
launched,
Shagging flies in right during batting
practice.
As I was comfortably camped under a
routine fly,
The proverbial “can of corn,” as the old
announcers used to say,
I was suddenly transfixed to see that
It wasn’t one baseball I was catching at
all
(The way I had always seen it before)
But two—the lighter side facing me that
was
Exposed to the sun and the darker half
That was in relative shade,
And suddenly somehow I felt the earth’s
roundness
*(O my Lord!)*
Not as an idea but as a reality, and
thought
Of people on the other side of the planet
For the first time, really, as people who
Are as alive as I am

And I thought of time stretching backward
and
Forward—and the human thought that
has
Existed in that history,
And I was filled with gratitude, strangely,
That in that moment I was there on the
earth
To catch that particular flyball

And nothing has ever been quite the same
since

(Go ahead and put that in your book)

Full disclosure: This is fiction—the acid droppers part. In fact, I've never dropped acid in my life, a little odd, even to me, given the full context of my life and the number of Dead concerts I attended. It's because of particular childhood feelings I'd had, described elsewhere in this book, which made a "bad trip" seem like it might be a genuinely terrifying experience that would go on for way too long.

I admit this request for my best baseball story, not the first communication I received from this person, who had been a batboy or clubhouse attendant for the Yankees decades earlier, sort of rubbed me the wrong way. But mainly it was the middle of the winter, I was in my mid-50's, in the late-middle of my teaching career, our kids grown and gone, and I was spending most evenings in my basement by the woodstove, thinking over what I would talk about with students the next day (I did enjoy teaching) and occasionally other things, walking outside every night to proclaim to the winter sky: "I step into the not merely illimitable, into the dear beautiful eternal night."

On one of those nights, perhaps because of this note, I was thinking about the old baseball days and that rather unusual feeling of noticing the shaded and unshaded sides of a flyball coming down for a landing in one's mitt. It was unusual because I caught so many flyballs and very rarely took note of how striking this actually looked.

So the joke, to me, or on me perhaps, is that it took 30 years to come to the understanding of this experience contained in the last few lines of the poem. I invented this story thinking maybe I could have saved myself a lot of time if I actually had just dropped some acid and shagged some flies. I did write a poem, or attempted poem, in the winter of '76 that began:

> I felt the earth's roundness today
> O my Lord!

## The Minor Leagues

Very few people seem to understand what the minor leagues are about and it's really not all that complicated so I want to try to explain some things about minor-league baseball.

The fundamental thing about minor-league baseball is that it is professional baseball. This has two important meanings. The first is that every minor leaguer gets paid a salary, although at the beginning it is truly meager. The set salary for every player starting out at the lowest level (Rookie League) when I first signed a contract in 1974 was $500 per month. This may sound ridiculously low but when I spoke recently to a friend and former teammate who is now coaching in a Class A League (the California League, actually a "high" A League) he thought salaries for his players averaged around $1000 per month, which probably does not go as far now in 1993 as $500 did in 1974. However, the point is that money is money and if you are playing in the minor leagues you are working under a "contract" with a major league team and are a professional baseball player. It's amazing how few people understand this—the inevitable question I must have heard 100 times in my minor league career, “When are you going to make the pros?” can really rankle. Although by the time I reached Triple A it, had acquired a kind of cult status as a clubhouse joke and caught rather nicely, to my way of thinking, the way in which baseball at that level can be an alternately exhilarating and humbling experience. That is, at the Triple A level players are in fact very close to being rich and famous and justifiably so (I should say justifiably so given that the whole system is not a joke and a sham) because the quality of play can be very high. However, making that next step to the Big Leagues can still be quite difficult and the procedure by which it happens can seem to be totally arbitrary so it is a perpetual roller-coaster ride. One moment you feel enormous confidence both in your game and your standing in an organization and the next you have just gone 0-16 in a four-game series in Des Moines and you find yourself in Des Moines International at six in the morning, having drunk way too much beer the night before in some effort to ward off the gods of 0-fers, looking at a three-stop flight to Evansville where you'll probably face some merciless, nasty lefthander in 12 hours and of course the waitress at the airport with whom you've struck up a conversation about baseball asks: “So what are your chances of ever making the pros?”

The second point is just that—however lowly your position in the minor leagues may be (and it can seem unspeakably low) it is still a continuum of professional baseball from the lowest Rookie League to the pinnacle of the Big Leagues. The disparity between making $500/month in Pulaski, Virginia, playing in front of maybe 200 people, and making several thousand dollars per at bat in Shea Stadium can be daunting but it is a gap that can be bridged in 2 or 3 years.

There is a second kind of confusing absurdity (I can't think of a better term) about playing in the minor leagues and it is that while it is frankly enormously difficult to get started in the minor leagues—to simply be offered a contract—the attrition rate for players who sign that contract is remarkably high.

It is reasonable to say that virtually anyone who is playing baseball in high school or college is in the pool of potential professional baseball draftees and yet each Major League team signs perhaps only 25-30 new players to a contract each year. This means that out of literally hundreds of thousands of amateur players (I don't mean to imply that all hope or want to play professional baseball) maybe 800 get an opportunity to play.

It should be obvious that nearly all of these new players have excelled at whatever level of amateur competition they have been engaged in (and that can vary tremendously—from a high-powered college program playing 60 games a year to someone coming from a small high school where he pitched 5 or 6 games each spring) and they bring a certain pride in themselves as "elite" athletes to their minor-league initiation.

But the terrible fact is that the funneling process has just begun—only 5 or 6% of all players who sign professional contracts ever make it to the Big Leagues—so that kids who have known only success in baseball find that their professional careers consist of a year or two of riding buses around the hinterlands while getting paid six or seven hundred dollars a month. It tends to take you down a peg or two.

Most Major League teams have four or five minor-league affiliates. Rookie League is the bottom of the heap—a half season starting in the middle of June and ending September 1—designed for new signees just coming out of high school or college. "A" ball is the next step up and is really the first true professional baseball season—six months long, counting spring training, and 144 games. Some teams have either two A teams (so that leagues are classified as High A, such as the California League, and Low A, such as the Western Carolina League) or two Rookie League teams. When I started with the Phillies they had two Rookie League teams and two A teams—this was quite rare. Then of course there is Double A and Triple A. I can't recall any organization having more or less than one team at each of these levels.

There is a tremendous pressure to produce at the Rookie League and A levels, although most players don't realize it until they are either released or have advanced to Double A. You can be released at any time although most players make it through the Rookie League season. From my Rookie League team, some were released over the next winter but most were invited to the next year's spring training. However, fully 2/3 of the players from my Rookie League team were released by the end of that spring training.

Rookie League is a trip. I played for the Pulaski Phillies in Pulaski, Virginia—the Appalachian League. The second week in June about 25-30 of us descended on Pulaski, Virginia, which probably none of us had ever heard of before, to embark on the dream. Maybe 1/2 were right out of high school, 1/4 were from Latin America (especially Puerto Rico, Venezuela, and the Dominican

Republic) and the rest of us from college or junior college. A large percentage of the American players came from California or Florida.

I had no idea what to expect when I got to Pulaski but I was quite impressed with the way things were set up. Granny Hamner, a former Whiz Kid with the Phillies, and Bob Tiefenauer, who I also knew had pitched in the Big Leagues, were there as instructors and our manager was Bob Wren, who had run a very successful program at Ohio University for a number of years.

There is a fascinating mix of talent at the Rookie League level and it is the very beginning of the one great inexorable process which sums up minor league baseball: dividing the prospects from the suspects. It is a fairly level playing field—whether or not you were drafted and your exact position in the draft (2nd round, 3rd round, etc.) definitely plays a part in how an organization views you at the outset but does not guarantee anything. For instance, I was not drafted at all but signed as a "free agent." This is the bottom of the totem pole but I had an exceptional Rookie League season, was invited to the Fall Instructional League where I played well, and by my first spring training had leap-frogged virtually everyone I started with to become a real "prospect".

The great exception to this is first-round draft choices, who really are different in terms of the treatment they receive. This is sometimes justified and sometimes not. The reasons are obvious. Major League organizations place enormous emphasis on identifying the elite of the elite and getting a good first-round pick. They are invariably scouted and re-scouted and cross-checked so it stands to reasons the selections will often be good ones. However, it is also true that organizations give far more in bonus money to first-round picks than anyone else, even second-rounders, and it often seems they go to great lengths to justify that investment.

I have very fond memories of that Rookie League season and it's not just because I played well. My wife and I fell in love that summer and she periodically flew down or drove down in her old van to see me and watch games. Quite frankly it was idyllic. I lived by myself in a large apartment in a big, old house for $85/month. When Patti came to visit she sometimes came to the games with her Great Dane in tow and sat on the grass down the left-field foul line. Sometimes she sat in the stands behind home plate where she eventually struck up a friendship with a middle-aged man named Vern who lived somewhere nearby in the country with his mother in a house with no running water. We corresponded with Vern for several years after that '74 season.

From Pulaski our team travelled for road games to Covington, Bluefield, Marion, Elizabethton, Kingsport, and Johnson City. I had no idea what to expect from this but as I began hitting home runs, gaining a kind of attention for that, and cementing my relationship with Patti, I can see now what a fundamental, future-setting time that was. I have no doubt it turned out that way precisely because I had no expectation about what was to come. It began almost as a lark.

I mentioned the fascinating mix of talent in Rookie League. Most of the players who played in the Appalachian League in 1974 were out of baseball within a year or two but we also had Lance Parrish, Dale Murphy, Mark Fidrych, Butch Wynegar, and a host of other future Big Leaguers playing with us.

To write about these players as I remember them—Butch Wynegar was obviously a very good player. He hit about .350 and looked very sound as a catcher. He was good fundamentally, had a nice business-like air about his game, and so on. Anyone could tell he was a good player but none of us could tell what that really meant about his prospects for getting to the Big Leagues, which he did very quickly and deservedly.

Mark Fidrych's rise was meteoric, of course. He was captivating the nation a year and a half after that '74 season. His antics in Detroit were no instant affectation—he was as goofy on the mound pitching in Pulaski with 100 people in attendance as he was later in the Big Leagues. Again it was impossible to tell in '74 how good he was. I faced him once or twice that summer and knew he had a good season but it wasn't as if anything could be projected from that.

Parrish and Murphy were very interesting that first season. Both were highly touted number 1 picks and neither one played very well, at least statistically. I frankly thought Murphy was a mistake when I first saw him play. He was drafted as a catcher and I thought he was too tall and skinny for the position. I also don't remember him hitting the ball hard all summer. But one day I watched him take infield practice before a game and I was simply mesmerized by the way he threw the ball. His motion was incredibly smooth and easy and yet his throws had a consistency and power that was simply beautiful. I watched and marveled the entire infield session trying to determine was his motion as easy and the flight of the ball as rapid as it seemed. I played against him the next season in A ball and he removed all doubt: he simply had the strongest arm I ever saw on a player. His second baseman that next year was 24 years old and had played a lot of baseball and sometimes on a steal attempt Murphy's throws from home plate would handcuff him. Sometimes also the centerfielder would catch them in the air. It was unbelievable.

I don't know how Lance Parrish remembers his initial season there in the Appalachian League but from the outside it looked like a fairly rough time for him. He was just out of high school and a very impressive-looking athlete—big and strong with a great arm—but I think he hit about .220. He was also a southern California boy and supposedly had been offered a scholarship to play quarterback at USC. He played third base that summer for the Bristol Tigers and an image I will always remember from a game in Pulaski one night was a routine grounder coming his way at third, taking a last second truly bizarre hop and plunking him on the side of the head, sounding fully as loud as a watermelon falling off a table. The ball was hit slowly but it landed so squarely he went down like a shot and the game was held up for a few minutes while he recovered. I don't know what he or anyone else was thinking but it occurred to me that if he ever questioned his decision not to run around in the Rose Bowl in front of 100,000 people in order to come to what must have seemed to him like the middle of nowhere and be attacked by harmless-looking grounders—it must have happened in that moment. It was like Achilles had been sent out to subdue some renegade pygmies and returned in disgrace.

I think there is a conventional wisdom that it is at the Double A level where players need to seriously establish themselves as having what it takes to play in the Big Leagues and I think that conventional wisdom is basically true. The most important thing about playing A ball is you have to get out of there—and fast in most cases although the time table varies according to whether a player is coming out of high school or college. A good college player, especially from a high-powered program, may well start at Double A, sometimes even Triple A. This can be a mixed blessing—there is still a pressure to produce quickly.

There are more factors at work in getting out of A ball than simply numbers or measurable success. A player with exceptional talent may be moved up in spite of relatively poor performance. This is entirely legitimate. Players mature at different rates and sometimes respond very positively to a challenge that on paper would seem to be over their heads. Also players may move up on the strength of a single talent which is unquestionably of Major League caliber even though the rest of their game lags far behind. For instance, Todd Cruz was a young shortstop with the Phillies when I started. He had a tremendous arm—he did stuff almost as amazing as Murphy—and he was the number 1 infield prospect in the Phillies organization. He moved up the ladder accordingly, quite independent of whether he hit .180 or .240 in the preceding season.

At the Double A level there is an increased emphasis on production. Prospects could become suspects in the absence of it and less frequently the opposite could happen—a player whose main purpose was to fill out a Double A roster or of whom not much was expected could draw some attention simply by putting up some numbers.

I suppose that on an average Double A team there are one or two players that an organization really pins some hope on and another five or six that they feel may blossom into Big Leaguers with some luck. But to say everyone else is just putting in their time would be wrong. Any one that produces has a chance to advance. This is not necessarily true in A ball. For instance, a player could put together a certain kind of fine season in an A league—hit around .300, steal 20 or so bases, catch everything hit his way, have a good attitude, score a lot of runs. But if that player is an outfielder and doesn't hit for power, even though he may be the most valuable player on that team, his chances of moving up may be very slim. There is good reason for this—none of that stuff necessarily projects to success at the Major League level. If your game is based on speed, it has to be Major League speed, which means you need to steal 50 or 60 bases and cover the outfield like a blanket. If it's based on hitting for average, .300 in A ball does not cut the mustard. It's almost a disadvantage to have a good attitude with those numbers. Strange as it may seem, you may be viewed as having more potential if you're not getting the most out of your talent yet.

It is difficult to classify the level of play in A ball, or compare it to anything else. Most good college teams could probably beat most A teams with a fair amount of consistency but that is really missing the point. A ball, as I said, revolves more around potential than production so the organizing principle that can make sense out of who is offered a contract initially, or why a Class A team might very legitimately play at a lower level than a college team composed entirely of players who would like to play professionally is that if you look closely at the A ballplayers you will probably find one skill at least that has the potential to be of Major League caliber.

You can see how nebulous this can be: an 18 year old drafted on the basis of his swing only may find under the uncompromising glare of a 144 game season that not only does the rest of his game remain sub-par but also that his swing doesn't develop or improve. He's out of the game before he knows what has hit him. It's very Darwinian.

The reverse can also happen. The faintest glimmer of talent at 18 can emerge over the next 2 or 3 years into really awesome ability—like blowing on an almost dead ember and starting a forest fire.

It is common in sports to speak of physical athletic talent and mental attitude as if they are separate aspects of an athlete's make up—to me it mirrors the genetics versus environment debate—and the shortcomings involved in looking at sports that way is highlighted for me when I think back on what it took for guys to make that "jump" from A ball to Double A.

On the one hand, the basic theme in who made it to Double A was simply what players had the most talent. An organization's decisions on this would probably be validated 9 times out of 10 by a clubhouse vote of players. But also in looking back

I think the crucial factor in who made it to Double A was what players adjusted successfully to the demands of playing professional baseball every day for 6 months.

Professional baseball in the lower minor leagues provides an interesting kind of psychological pressure. Players who have been elite athletes in their hometowns now find themselves at the bottom of what can seem like an immensely high ladder. The pay is poor, the lights and field conditions can be inferior to an average college facility, and of course there are the bus rides.

But what I think is most challenging is the simple fact of playing every day. It is different and more difficult than playing a lot of games in an amateur situation because there is really nothing else psychologically to fall back on when things are going poorly. If you go 3-20 in A ball, you can't take solace in how much money you are making or what you accomplished previously in professional baseball (as a Major Leaguer can or even a player in Triple A can) nor can you take solace in your Business major or the general knowledge that after all you are pretty much doing this for fun as a college player can.

The point I am trying to make is that in retrospect the early weeding out process in professional baseball has as much to do with who does not adapt to the game psychologically as who does not have the physical talent. It's a fairly subtle adaption I am talking about and it boils down to this: You have to learn how to minimize slumps and maximize hot streaks.

What does it mean to minimize a slump? A slump (as, for instance, a bad week—say 3-28) can screw up a player psychologically. It can wreck his self-image or self-esteem as a ball player and destroy his workaday approach to each game. In other words, when you do your level best time after time with no results, if you don't "have what it takes," a natural response is at some level to back off a little bit, to build up defenses about why you are failing. In short, to protect yourself. It's a kind of death. I believe it happens and some players finish out an entire season, play for 2 or 3 months at a time, at this lower level of commitment.

The way a player can damage himself physically in a slump is by making drastic adjustments to his game—in effect, doing or trying anything—to come out of it. For instance in hitting, for me it was enormously tempting to "wrap" the bat (tilt it slightly toward the pitcher) when things aren't going well. It's hard to explain but it simply gives you an illusion of power, a feeling of security, and may occasionally result in a long home run. But it's the wrong path to take, inevitably limiting success, while only seeming to limit the downside possibilities.

Professional baseball is certainly about developing your talent but to a large extent what that ultimately means is simply letting your talent come out. Most professional baseball players are not going to make it to the Big Leagues, no matter what they do. Many players actually decrease their chances for success out of a simple fear of failure.

Interestingly enough, some players also have a hard time handling success. If they start a game with a home run or 2 hits in their first 2 at-bats, they almost visibly check out for the rest of the game. In some cases they literally check out. Some guys will go 2 for 2 and their hamstrings get tight or a pitcher with 5 innings in and a comfortable lead will look for the hook.

Maybe you can see where I am going with this: Professional baseball mirrors in a very physical, prosaic way a spiritual journey where you have to drop everything—your attachment to success and failure, your favorite ideas—and just do the work. What is interesting then is that when you become freer and freer from all those ideas, you have less choice about things in some ways. There is only one right way for you to prepare for a game (this is not rigid, it varies every day). There is only one way (your particular way) to field a ground ball. It's very simple about whether you should have swung at a given pitch or not. This is a very clean process. It's the main thing I got out of playing baseball. But what is extremely interesting is that what develops at the same time, whether as an undesirable side effect or an inevitability or what, is that the addiction to playing professional baseball begins to kick in.

It's enormously paradoxical: on the one hand, you are freeing yourself up from a lot of psychological crap; on the other, you find there is really only one way for you to do things and you become addicted to the whole process.

I'm going far afield now of what I intended to write about in this part so I just want to throw out a few random thoughts here and maybe come back to these ideas later or develop them more thoroughly in another context. Random thought No. 1: The implication of what I've been saying up to this point is that it's not a very happy situation. Players who come out of professional baseball without having made it and with their protective mechanisms and "false" self-esteem intact (that is, those who have kept the game at arm's length, been released, and gone on to bigger and better things possibly with the same approach—the idea being that this approach works in the "real world") have really missed the point. However, those who have gotten the point as I have presented it find themselves addicted to a kids' game which they are forced to leave cold turkey (via being released) if unsuccessful. Or if successful they may wind up with significant earnings but find themselves statistically at a pretty high risk of suicide, divorce, substance abuse, etc., when their glory days (addiction) are over.

Random thought No. 2: This idea of keeping the game at arm's length, not getting the point of it, can manifest in a lot of ways. It boils down to trying to find security in a very unstable situation. Or trying to make concrete, understandable, and logical a process which is as illogical and unstable as time and human achievement and human error. For example, in A ball, guys on shaky ground may try to find solace in statistics. If you look at their overall game what they should be worried about is that with their arm, speed, and power they have to do remarkable things to even be a longshot for making it. Instead they will worry about their statistics in this way: Are they hitting .260 or .280? As if some number will guarantee something. It's hard to express the meaningless—it can almost make you crazy just thinking about it - of someone sitting in a hotel room in Lynchburg in August trying to project what they will have to do to finish the season at .280. But I've seen it happen.

Here's the best example I can give of what I mean. My first full year ('75) was in A ball. My roommate had signed the year before, played in a Rookie League, and gone to the Instructional League—a good start. He was a catcher and was then invited to the Major League spring training that spring of '75 as a non-roster player. This is a real and important status symbol but one which is often extended to catchers. They serve as glorified bullpen assistants for two or three weeks in spring training so all the pitchers can get their work in. Still it was an important feather in his cap.

What I will always remember is that one day early in the regular season he tried to explain what it meant to his career to have been in "Big League Camp". It went like this: "Yeah, having been in Big League Camp after just half a season, it probably means I could have a bad season this year, go to spring training next year and still not do anything, and I still probably wouldn't get released." Even then, when I had just started and didn't have much of a different attitude myself, the way he said it gave me the heebie-jeebies. He did play badly that season and the next spring training. In my view this was very definitely a self-fulfilling prophecy. But he was wrong about the security. He was released after that spring training, exactly a year after the pinnacle of going to the Major League camp.

I can't believe I've written this much about the minor leagues without getting out of A ball yet, so to speak, but an idea I hinted at earlier leads naturally into exploding a conventional wisdom or two, which is probably my favorite pastime.

The idea is this: What you learn in playing professional baseball is that you have to drop all your reflexes, mechanisms, and strategies that people typically employ in the face of failure to protect their self-esteem. I take that to be something desirable in itself and difficult to do but ball players don't do it because they want to or because they have achieved spiritual insight. They do it because it is necessary in order to get the most out of their talent. I think this is a kind of unspoken code that ball players figure out on their own—a trial and error process of discovering what works and what doesn't. This is the great thing about the difficulty of playing professional baseball. You get direct feedback not only on your techniques but also on your overall approach to playing. I mean here only half-jokingly (or not really joking at all) the Tao of baseball.

I also have the idea that most Americans don't get this kind of feedback, that they can't see such a direct relationship between their success and failure and the way they go about doing things.

The conventional wisdom I present to support these ideas is this: I mentioned at the beginning of this part about the minor leagues that most people seem to have no idea what minor league baseball is about. There are two exceptions to this. I have always been struck by the frequency with which people have identified two negative things about the minor leagues: The bus rides are terrible and "politics" rule the decision-making process in terms of who advances, or makes it to the Big Leagues, and who is released.

Bus rides are certainly a drag, but the main thing they are is simply part of the job. In any baseball season, half the games are played at home, half on the road. Road games are usually played in four-game stands which means that in a minor league season half of the time on every fourth night after a game you ride a bus. When I played in A ball the average distance was between 3 and 4 hours. In the Eastern League, where I played Double A, it could be worse. We made 2 or 3 swings from Reading up to Canada each year which was about 10-12 hours each way. This can definitely give you a headache but professional baseball presents one very profound challenge—making it to the Major Leagues—and if healthy young men are serious about finding out if they can do that, riding on a bus 20 nights a year probably shouldn't stand in the way.

What you have to learn in the minor leagues is how to do your best every night, whether you've been riding on a bus the night before, or been up all night with a sick baby, or had a fight with your girlfriend, or whatever. So if you can't handle going 0-4 after a bus ride, you blame it on the bus ride. This is not the way.

Similarly about politics. Guys who lose out in one way or another to someone else competing for a position often blame it on "politics", which means that the people making decisions simply liked the other guy better. Sometimes of course there is some truth in this but more often it is self-indulgent. What "politics" means is that the people making decisions don't judge you the way your mother would judge you (or you would judge yourself).

Bus rides and politics are a part of baseball, a negative part of baseball, but to assert they are predominant in determining what the experience is like is a cop-out. Again, what is striking is how quickly people outside of baseball latch onto these aspects of the game as something important.

## Baseball Dream II

A good friend from baseball days was Bobby DeMeo, exactly my age, coming out of college after four years at the University of Northern Colorado, the same year I graduated from Duke. Neither one of us was highly heralded—four-year college players kind of an anomaly in those days. We played together at Oklahoma City in 1979, and were also together the next year when he went into coaching, starting right there in OKC where I also returned as a player.

He was an East Coast guy, of Italian descent, but it was his wife Claire that had more the bubbly, effervescent personality—they were really a fun couple to be around, for both my wife Patti and me.

Around Christmas, 1981, the last year I played, we were spending the winter in northern Washington and received word that Bobby had been killed by a drunk driver in Denver, where he and Claire lived. I ended my playing career just before the start of spring training in '82 and consequently seldom if ever talked with fellow, former teammates about Bobby's tragic passing.

The next fall I began studies at the Kototama Institute in Santa Fe—traditional acupuncture, the

Kototama Principle, and so forth. Claire came for a visit, really struggling, by her own description. I gave her the kind of handwork treatment I was learning then, acupressure, you might say, though that's not quite accurate. It's hard to explain, hard even for me to relate to now in my old age, how clearly I could feel her pain, though helpless really to do anything about it.

After she left I had this dream: It was Bobby's funeral, being held in the junior high gym/auditorium in the old school I grew up next to and attended. This gym/auditorium space was already old-fashioned in the early 60's. The new gym was just downstairs from this one, so that it was a strangely nostalgic place for me in those early years, coming up the back stairs from the new gym to emerge into an earlier time, so to speak. It still is. I came to northern Michigan to teach and coach 25 years ago when my own kids were entering middle school, and there were still some of these old gyms in use.

My dream started in the new gym and somehow moved upstairs to the auditorium now filled with chairs and people in attendance for the funeral. A song was playing—an old Van Morrison tune. I was crazy for Van Morrison in those days—a topic for a separate baseball essay that may make its way into this book. But this was strange and almost funny—the song that was filling the auditorium was one of maybe only two songs in Van's catalogue I actively disliked, could barely listen to. The title is "It's Alright," from the early days of his recording career, and I always found the guitar riff or lead-in genuinely grating. Now it seemed beautiful and what was particularly beautiful were the back-up singers—The Sweet Inspirations—singing "It's Alright." But what really filled the auditorium, more even than the song, was Bobby's spirit, alive in real time after his death assuring me and everyone else in the most wonderful way that it—our common fate—really is alright.

I awoke with the dream fresh and powerful in my head and immediately played the song—I'm pretty sure I had all his records in those days—and it sounded as powerful and beautiful, especially the guitar, as it had in my dream, and made me weep—for Bobby and all the rest of us. It still does sound powerful and beautiful to me.

A couple weeks later in his regular Monday night lecture, Sensei said: "Until you have cried for the fate of every human being, you cannot be a real human being." I gave a silent but heartfelt Amen to that one.

*December, 2023*

## Final Notes on Baseball

I find in my old age there just isn't much more I care to write about baseball. There are moments that still stand out—sitting in the stands with Bob Johnson and Freddie Beene in 1977 along the first-base side for a day game in Des Moines with Joe Lis, who played for Des Moines. There had been a storm the night before and although the sun was shining, the field was clearly unplayable and the game about to be called, and Joe was telling Roger Freed stories. (Example: Roger hits a deep drive to left and immediately goes into his home run trot. Ball hits the fence and Roger is thrown out easily at second, not even a slide. Manager Frank Lucchesi is already yelling at Roger as he reaches the dugout steps. Roger: "Goddammit, Frank, that ball's out in Rochester!")

And this connects to sitting on a bus next to Ted Simmons on the way to a Brewers' spring training game in 1981 and Simmons telling Roger Freed stories. Ted Simmons was the most interesting superstar I ever met, and he said several of the most interesting things I ever heard anybody say about playing professional baseball. A couple of them I just read in the newspaper. "The secret to playing in the big leagues is to reach a high level of motivation and stay there". And on hitting: "When it's not going well, I just need to take batting practice until I get the feel of it again". And to me on that bus ride, about hitting: "If a pitcher throws you a breaking ball and you got less than two strikes, spit on it." That was interesting also because Enos Slaughter used to say exactly the same thing to Duke ballplayers in the early 70's about his days in the big leagues decades earlier. I talked about this when I talked to the Duke baseball team in the fall of 2018. It felt good to tell those young players an idea about hitting major-league pitching that was true for two great hitters whose careers covered such a large portion of the 20th century.

And then finally, something I heard from Mike Anderson when we played together in OKC, from his days with Simmons in St. Louis, the greatest thing I ever heard a hitter say about hitting: "0-2 (a count of no balls and two strikes) is not a problem. He still has to throw you a strike". People tend to forget, I think, that for at least a few years in the 70's Ted Simmons was perhaps the most feared and respected hitter in the National League. I just really liked that a guy at that level, facing the greatest pitchers in baseball, could feel that kind of confidence—and put it into words.

I really only have a couple basic thoughts or ideas about professional baseball in the 21st century. First and foremost, the money is just too much. There was a breaking point for me in the 90's when salaries went over two million dollars a year. It's not some kind of economic philosophy, unless maybe you can be a two-million-dollar-a-year communist. It's just on the face of it, in the whole scheme of things, nah, I'm sorry, that's too much.

And then there is something that is interesting to me related to this, a conclusion I've reached over the last few years. The players may have been wage slaves in the old days—the owners making millions and balking at paying the players thousands—but in another real sense it was the players who owned the game. The "Book" for playing professional baseball in the old days was a real thing, and it was written by the players themselves and the coaches and managers who had almost exclusively also been players. And this book would change as the game evolved—the clearest change to me was when the Gene Mauch-style of baseball basically was replaced by the Earl Weaver-style.

But now that the teams are worth billions and the players are making millions, it just seems to me that strangely it's no longer the players' game. It's very hard for me to wrap my head around this, but I think it is true: They're paying you $30 million a year to play ball—they own you.

Or perhaps it's just another version of the end of *Animal Farm*, owners and players alike sitting together at the Great Table Greed, fans not admitted for batting practice at one stadium, paying $20 or $50 or $100 for a hot dog and a coke at another.

I blame *Moneyball.*

And finally, you might have noticed in a couple baseball poems the references to the One hand clapping koan. These references don't go back originally to my deep studies of Zen, although I have over the years read and taken seriously and enjoyed *Three Pillars of Zen*, and *Zen Mind, Beginner's Mind*, and still enjoy especially *Zen Flesh, Zen Bones*.

But the source of those references in the poems goes back quite a bit earlier. I was just one of those kids that was grateful for the voice he heard in *The Catcher in the Rye*. And then I was a kid that would track down and read whatever else I could find by Salinger, usually with a certain level of disappointment, but seeing "What is the sound of one hand clapping" on the introductory page to *Nine Stories* stayed with me. So there is a certain level of youthful, lighthearted self-deprecation with the conclusion of "Baseball Enlightenment". Frankly it began as a bit of a joke at my own expense: Brother, you want to hear the sound of one hand clapping, you should have seen me that time at the Vet...

I did get more serious about it as I went along, I mean in the writing of it, and by the time I got to the Astroturf and Josh Gibson part, I was quite serious about it, in a good way. If I've written any poems, I count that as one of them. I think a lot of good things start that way.

But then a sort of surprising thing came out of my own writing. The second paragraph at the very beginning of this book *(The through-line in all my writing...)* did just come to me spontaneously when I was trying to write the story of a meadowlark out in South Dakota. This was in 2021. What I realized very quickly was that "Visions, dreams, poems, experience, prayer" was a kind of taxonomy for me, first for my writing, and then pretty much my whole life. Experience contains rational thought. Prayer is the sound practice which I had come to believe more than anything else enables, empowers, activates our innate capacity for the visions, dreams, and poems.

To me, here's the really funny part. An answer to the question—What is the sound of one hand clapping?—also just came to me out of the blue, at least as well as I recall, one moment in the early 90's when we were living in Boulder. I remember exactly where I was in our modest home, the hall from the bedrooms to the living room, when it just hit me: The sound of one hand clapping is human thought—the only unresonant thing in the universe.

I still like that, it makes sense to me, and I think a big part of our problem today is that we are bound or limited by the parameters of rational thought, coming from our experience, through the physical senses, of the physical world.

And once again, I'm not coming at this originally as some kind of New Age Aquarian throwback or whatever, but just as an athlete. It was a little frustrating to me in the old days how frequently reporters would ask, "So what were you thinking when..." If Yogi Berra never said this, he should have: Sometimes thinking is a stupid thing to do. But this doesn't only apply to sports. I hope to make this clear in the second part of the book, but for me the best way to shut off the too-much-rational-thought problem and allow or open oneself up to other aspects of this marvelous existence, aside perhaps from being a ballplayer, is to go out in a meadow somewhere....

# *Interlude*

[illegible] answer "my mother is dead"

(1)

I was [illegible] the streets of a city
When [illegible] brought to my eye
The children were young and handsome
And their misery made misery
I noticed one in particular
With cheeks that were fiery red
I asked him what was the matter
His answer "my mother is dead"

(2)

I said ~~th~~ to him to ha[illegible]age
And face the wide wor[illegible]ight
Be good and ~~[illegible]~~ [illegible]ld me
His dear mother
In a land where there [illegible]ight
but his fond heart was [illegible]
and the lines on his face I rea[illegible]
But I can't help thinking the [illegible]
his answer "my mother is dead"

Composed by J. [illegible]

March 8th 1898

## Coincidence

In the first week of March in 1968, my mother suffered a stroke. I was 15 and a sophomore in high school then, and with my dad we had all taken a light jog, a few blocks around the neighborhood in the early evening. It was intended to be for my mother the start of one of those periods of "getting back in shape" so many adults, including myself, initiate in middle-age.

She had a history of migraines and felt bad almost immediately upon getting back to the house. We had a small landing on the way upstairs and I remember her laying there, legs draped down across the first few steps right after we got back. Things deteriorated pretty rapidly over the next hour or so, me asking repeatedly if it was beginning to get better yet, until it became obvious we needed to call for help. She was lapsing into a coma, from which she never recovered, as the ambulance arrived. I do remember the last few words she spoke, a complete sentence but not entirely making sense, as she left. She died three days later in the early morning hours of March 8.

We were a small but I would say very close family. The day after the funeral our grandmother showed us this poem which our grandfather had written in 1898:

His answer "my mother is dead"

I was walking the streets of a city
When sorrow was brought to my eye
The children were young and handsome
And their misery made me cry
I noticed one in particular
With cheeks that were fiery red
I asked him what was the matter
His answer "my mother is dead"

I said to him to have courage
And face the wide world so bright
Be good and he would meet his dear mother
In a land where there is no night
but his fond heart was in sadness
and the lines on his face I read
But I can't help thinking the words
his answer "my mother is dead"

Composed by JG Kraner
March 8, 1898

The fundamental coincidence of my life is this poem by my grandfather composed 70 years to the day before my mother's death. Like dreams, I don't have a particular theory about coincidence one way or another, but some of them pack a particular kind of punch, in my experience, and this is the bedrock of that feeling for me.

Not that the immediate impact was so great. I always remembered seeing this poem that morning, but I don't remember any of us ever talking about it together. In fact, over the years I lost track of the exact day of her death, unable to remember if it was the 8th or the 12th for some reason until in the mid 80's I mentioned this to my sister-in-law who gave me a pneumonic device—the 8th in '68—that stayed with me. But a couple years later I talked with my uncle about the poem and he sent me this copy of it. There was no real backstory. My grandfather passed away in 1957 after suffering a stroke himself a few years earlier. They found this poem in an old trunk after his death, with no accompanying words of explanation or any other poems, which of course only made it that much more interesting and even powerful for me.

My mother was a good, strong, vibrant person. I want to write here what I still think of as my first poem, if ever in fact I have written a real poem:

> Mother, mother, dead 7 years,
> Who am I talking to?

I always thought as a child there were times other kids were clearly "talking to" one or more of the adults that had influenced them, usually a parent. Certainly I was, almost always my mom.

More than 40 years later, in response to a conversation with my sister, I wrote this haiku, which I "published" on facebook on the 50th anniversary of my mother's death:

> Do I remember
> Her voice? Her voice is the pond
> Upon which I skate.

And then finally this poem, written on March 8, 2019, which I think of as my last baseball poem, and not incidentally also about coffee, but mainly a poem for my mother, and then everyone else:

March 8, 2019

Boy I tell you what
(as Buck, who attended Rocky Mount
        Philies games
in '75—the old Carolina League—used to
        say:
"Boy I tell you what."
"What?"
"Son, I just told you."
"Oh.")
I say, Boy I tell you what—
when you haven't had a cup of coffee
since December and you finished
7 weeks of chemo-radiation
3 weeks ago,
and for whatever it is worth
the prognosis is...hopeful,
like the coming Spring,
and you finally feel like a cup
would once again be a real pleasure,
it is something else to go outside

on a freezy cold but beautiful
March morning—March 8
to be exact—51 years to the day
after Mary Ellen's passing—
and get that old cup of coffee pleasure,
remembering the vacation in Canada
in 1960, a rustic cabin on a small lake,
sitting in the lodge after breakfast,
the little child me anxious to get going,
my mother saying, "I like to linger
over my coffee."
Yes, dear Mother, let's,
on this plane and the next.
You and cancer have taught me two great
things:
Death is real and this fine day is enough.

So here's to you, Mom,
and my old friend Vukovich
who passed 12 years ago today
and my childhood friend Greg Bair,
who died 2 years ago today,
who friended me on facebook
and who I never reached out to
(how I regret that)
and then of course to everyone,
I'm pouring a little coffee on the ground to
the West,
as my friend out West taught me,
and sharing this cup

# *Vision 2*

# Foreword

It is axiomatic to say that the basic sounds of the human voice, the sounds we use to create language, are in themselves meaningless. I don't recall ever seeing this fundamental premise challenged, outside the confines of the Kototama Institute in Santa Fe decades ago. This is interesting to me, first as an old English major, because it is also axiomatic that great poetry needs to be read aloud to be fully appreciated. And it is interesting also, it seems to me, because a great number of serious and intelligent people express affection, admiration, and even love for one particular language or another.

For me personally, this is more than just interesting. I have spent some 40 years investigating the possibility that the basic sounds humans articulate may just have inherent or intrinsic meaning after all. I am reminded of the old gag about the difference between being involved and committed. It's as simple as ham and eggs. The chicken is involved; the pig is committed. I am committed on this question, not that the sounds are in fact meaningful in themselves, but simply that it is a matter worthy of investigation.

Here is a basic guide to the second part of this book. After my baseball career ended in 1981, I became a student at the Kototama Institute in Santa Fe, studying acupuncture and other related topics. I was a licensed acupuncturist for ten years. In my early 40's, I got a Master's Degree in Secondary English Education and became a schoolteacher. One night in 2007, I received a phone call from a former student. One thing led to another and I had a vision relating to those earlier studies and the fairly immediate future.

In brief, this vision was an absolute certainty that the world was going to change for the better in 2011. So the second half of this book was embedded in time, you might say, from the very start. Here's an example of what I mean. I created a website called Intimations of 2011. It became absolutely essential to me to get that website up and running and to take a public stand, before 2011.

I still look at the things from late 2007 through 2011, both my state of mind and the writing, as something somehow separate and inviolate. An example that seems almost funny to me now: I needed help setting up the website, and I got very anxious about getting the rights to Intimations of

2011 as a website address. Not only was I quite certain the change was coming, not only was I quite certain other people would be feeling it, I was pretty sure the connection to the Wordsworth poem would become as patently clear to at least a few other people as it was to me.

At the beginning of this book, I said if the Donnie Moore essay didn't still hold up, I wouldn't have a book. In a related way, I felt certain also that if I hadn't made a record, publicly, before 2011 about the things I was thinking and feeling about the days to come, once again, there wouldn't be a book here. This is what I mean about embedded in time.

And in all honesty, as I hope to make clear in these pages, it has been that kind of ongoing process ever since.

One further note about the introductory essay: part of the reason it took me more than a year to write was I just couldn't figure out how to sound rational and serious and record the part about the numbers and the date and the spine—12/17. When I finally got the one incredibly long sentence out all in one piece, it was sort of cathartic. When I contacted people after posting this first essay online, the nearly universal response was...silence. For various reasons, I thought it might have been that one sentence, above all else, that was a deal-breaker.

No one wanted to call me crazy, which I did expect from at least one person, but a real response taking that sentence into account was somehow out of the question.

I came to think of it as my flaming sword sentence—readers just couldn't get past it. It was never my intent to be difficult or long-winded or obscure, so to have a sentence with 163 words was hardly a goal. But I found I simply could not change it. This brings another metaphor to mind, one I've heard is in use among jazz musicians: you gotta eat pork to hit a flatted fifth. I think of that one long sentence as my flatted fifth. It took me over a year to get to it, and it's gonna remain intact.

*15 March 2009*

## Vision 2: Intimations of 2011

On December 17, 2007, I received a phone call from Will S., a former student. He had graduated from the school where I teach, joined the Army, and was calling from Germany where he was then stationed before his scheduled deployment to Iraq the next spring.

It's not unusual for teachers to receive calls like this. I nearly always enjoy them, although, coming at random times, it can be a little like having your personal and professional reflexes played with. I have to remind myself it's not too crucial what I say. Either they want to talk about something specific or they want to talk in general. After you figure that out, it's mainly a matter of being a good listener.

This turned out to be just a good, friendly conversation. We talked about some of his adventures on leave in Europe. At some point it occurred to me it was either very early or very late in Germany (about 7:30 where I live in America) but it didn't seem to me as if he had been drinking, as I might have been at his age making a similar kind of phone call.

We also talked quite a bit about his training in Germany and eventually got around to his scheduled Iraq deployment. He told me his job there would be to drive around in a vehicle designed to detect and disarm IED's. Students often like to tell teachers things they don't want to say to other adults, like their parents, so you always have to be prepared to hear about traumatic break-ups or unwanted pregnancies and so forth. They're expecting you to remain calm—it's part of the reason they're talking to a teacher—but I have to admit as the nature of Will's mission became clear to me, I had kind of an inner *Casablanca* moment: "Holy shit! Of all the jobs in all the...." I did, however, manage to keep it together for the rest of our conversation. At one point he talked about a cutting-edge new vehicle the Army was developing not only to withstand the average IED but with an outer shell which, if hit by extraordinarily large bombs, would shatter in pieces and fall to the ground, leaving intact the inner core of a functioning vehicle. His description painted an extremely vivid picture in my mind.

We talked for half an hour or so, a good conversation by any standard—between teacher and former student, young adult and older guy, or just two friends.

Later that evening, I was hanging out in the kitchen, leaning against the counter listening to music, thinking things over as I usually do in the evenings, probably getting ready to check the woodstove in the old farmhouse where we live, when I had the strongest sensation I've ever had in my life—physical, mental, spiritual—whatever levels there are or I can experience.

The feeling itself was pretty simple, although it will take a while to explain the background and context. It was simply that 2011 is coming. What 2011 means to me, aside from being an arbitrary calendar date, is the time a number of different cultural or spiritual traditions have predicted will usher in a new and better level of human consciousness.

I first heard this idea when I began studying Oriental medicine and the Kototama Principle with Sensei M. Nakazono in Santa Fe in 1982. But it's been a widely discussed idea, even in mainstream culture, for quite a while. Shortly after hearing Sensei talk about it, I read a blurb in *Mother Earth News,* of all places, about the Mayan Calendar and Mayan prophecies about 2011. It was the idea behind the widely-publicized Harmonic Convergence in 1987. Even good old Jerry Garcia talked about this in his last interview with *Rolling Stone* (sometimes, as I think was true in this case, the year 2012 is cited instead of 2011. I don't know why).

But the feeling I had on December 17th wasn't an idea. It was a concrete certainty that in 2011 things will be different. I want to try to describe that certainty. I think I'm a pretty normal person. I have an okay record of academic achievement and I fool around with writing a little bit, but I also used to be an athlete and the fact is those kinds of experiences—the simple physical reality of my own body—are a very basic thing with me. And that is where this sensation began. It wasn't a vision from the stars, rather quite the contrary. It seemed to come from the earth through my toes and spine and culminate in the most interesting kind of tingling sensation at the base of my neck. As I said, in many ways I'm a very simple kind of physical person and I've thought since that simple physical things were a big part of this moment. I've been living and growing food in the place where this happened for more than a dozen years. My son and I the summer before had laid down a Spanish tile floor in the kitchen, and the counter I was leaning against had been built by a friend of mine from an oak tree that had been logged nearby.

I'm well aware all that may sound more than a little goofy (what about this whole thing, or existence in general when you get right down to it, doesn't?), but the simple fact is I was intensely aware at the time of where I was on the earth.

There isn't a whole lot more to say about that moment. I almost feel like a semi-cosmical, totally comical Paul Revere with one simple message: 2011 is coming! 2011 is coming! Just about the only conscious thought I had was an image related to my conversation with Will—2011 is coming like a missile that will hit the fake outer shells of our personalities which will then shatter and fall to the ground, leaving our authentic human cores intact.

I don't know how long this moment lasted, more than a minute certainly, less than five I'm pretty sure. The only cognitive action I had was the personality-shattering image. No self-monitoring whatsoever, which is most unusual for me. Also, when the moment ended, no sense of regret or control, just that it was over. Again, I am not that kind of person. All I felt was a vague sense of gratitude and some astonishment. I walked into our bathroom, which adjoins the kitchen, where my wife was taking a shower with both the door and bathroom window open, as has been her custom for the 35 years we have lived together, and said to the shower curtain: "I think I just woke up."

I'm 56 years old and have been around the block a few times. I knew what I was doing when I said that. To me when someone says: “I’m in love with her,” the best days of that relationship are over. More seriously, as soon as a Christian says out loud: “I’m born again,” he isn’t born again any more. But in this case the moment had ended as naturally as it came and I wanted to say out loud, set a kind of peg in time, in full normally-skeptical consciousness mode, just how remarkable a moment it had been.

There was one aftershock later in the evening. I was discussing the experience at some length with my wife and my daughter (our daughter, 21 at the time, was home from college for Christmas) both of whom were familiar with the intellectual backdrop of the idea of a coming sea-change in human consciousness but even more than me probably didn’t have the faintest idea what to think of this particular business, when I said out loud, almost but not quite in a joking tone of voice: “I want somebody to write this down: On 12-17” seeing the numbers in my head as I said it (I see all the words as I am speaking, a strange quirk so that I can say words backwards as easily as forwards, not phonetically but as they are spelled) but in this case I saw the numbers themselves,12-17, in my mind I had a long, slow, altogether pleasant and smiling moment: “Oh yeah 5-7 5-5-7.” I’ve had moments like that before, two or three times, but this was something else altogether. Coincidence and irony and an inexhaustible source for meditation all coming together at once, a long, sunny slope opening slowly out onto a beautiful vista. In all of literature, and I was a serious English major when English majors still read a lot, and have continued those studies, the only thing I know that was anything like this experience was when Odysseus would "laugh in his heart". As I recall, this would always be during some time of crisis when suddenly a path would open up that with hard work and facing down danger just might lead to success. It wasn't success itself but just a shifting of the insurmountable odds slightly in his favor.

Now this business of the 5-7 5-5-7 will take some 'splaining and connects directly to the old days at the Kototama Institute, but not my studies with Sensei Nakazono. Instead it connects to the sound meditation class taught there by a saintly old guy named Hikalu. Sensei Nakazono was the most authentic and compelling personality I've ever known, but I need to make it crystal-clear that as big an influence as he has been on my life, I claim no understanding of the real sense of his teachings about the Kototama Principle. I still read his books but the fact I must face is I still don't know my *a priori* from my *a posteriori*, still have no understanding of the innate differences in meanings of the particular sounds.

Hikalu's sound class met two mornings a week at the old dojo on Alto Street, Tuesdays and Thursdays from 8:00 to 8:30. I attended religiously for three years until it ended when the school closed. Attendance ranged widely over the years from as many as 10-15 at a time to a core group of three or four of us near the end. Two of these were the best friends I made in my time at the Institute, although now I haven't spoken to either of them in over 20 years. I had no expectations for the class, never any real understanding about what we were doing, but strangely now look back at those years of sound class as one of the seminal experiences of my life. The whole deal of the 12-17 thing is a separate tab, my next entry on this site, but there's no particular mystery about it. It has to do with practicing the free sounds, and the human spine, and Hikalu's sound class, his own eternal "Ta!" more often than not beginning the free sounds and ringing through the sacred old dojo and the crystal-clear air of Santa Fe in the early 1980's, and then it has to do maybe with the earth and the moon and the stars. But it has taken me a year to get just this much up and this site is ultimately about common people like myself feeling inside themselves that a change is coming, and I would feel pretty silly if I couldn't get my website up about 2011 being on its way until after 2011 has arrived.

Not that I haven't been working on it. The only other remotely conscious feeling I had during my epiphany of December 17th was that change was coming from the west. Either then or later that night, and this is the only part of the experience that is intellectually murky for me, I had something like certainty that it was coming specifically from South Dakota. That doesn't sound as strange to me as it probably does to you, but still, I was more than a little skeptical. Nevertheless, because the experience was so compelling, or because I am completely nuts, or whatever, I drove out on the Plains by myself last summer to try to write down what I was thinking and feeling about things. I wound up spending five nights in Mobridge, South Dakota where I watched the sun rise three mornings in a row from Sitting Bull's grave overlooking the Missouri River and returned to my room to write feverishly, 60-70 pages, which I haven't looked back at yet,

On the way back home, I spent the night in Steele, North Dakota, at a terrific little place you have to drive in to town to find. It was the best, cheapest room I stayed in on the whole trip. I walked around the town that night for exercise and it was the spookiest small town I've ever been in, not a single sign of life anywhere on the streets or behind closed curtains (this was around nine o'clock) until I bumped into a fellow schoolteacher who was walking her dog. We talked for 10-15 minutes about the things schoolteachers talk about—local cultures, funding issues, retirement plans—but when I got back to my clean, quiet room, I had a restless night, wondering as always what I was doing, what I had been doing.

The next morning I stopped early for gas and coffee at a place on the Interstate. It was as cold and impersonal as you can get in the middle of nowhere—recorded advertising blaring at the pumps, a dozen coffee machines inside to pick from. But I noticed as I went inside a couple of old farmers standing on the curb at the far end of the store, drinking coffee and staring at the distant horizon with the eternal wistfulness of white men on the prairie, trying to remember to wonder why they had fucked up such a beautiful country. As I was leaving with my own cup of coffee they were still there and a younger man, obviously a farmer also, walked up behind them and spoke the most perfectly comic Zen-joke I have ever heard: "That's

North!" I chuckled all the way to my car and drove over to them on my way out and rolled down my window and said: "I couldn't help but overhear you fellers. I'm not from around here. If that's north, what direction would that be?" extending my arm out the open window. The young farmer Zen master was puzzled by my unexpected idiocy and said: "Oh, no, that's west," but I was still chuckling as I drove off and by the time I reached the end of the parking lot wished I had replied: "Why thank you boys! That's the direction I'm headed. I've got a very important meeting in New York City—a matter of life and death—and I've got to be there by noon."

As I got on the Interstate, headed east, of course, I drove into a perfect morning sunrise and had a Kerouac-satori just outside Steele, North Dakota. I pulled over on the side of the Interstate and wrote down the story of it, weeping. I haven't reread that page either yet, but in my mind it still shimmers, and I felt like the goofiest Jack Mormon in Utah coming in from the remotest part of the desert claiming to have found the Golden Leaves, feeling that for once in my life, on this trip, I had actually nailed it.

But now it's 2009 already. My ideas about free sounds and all the rest of it will have to wait. My current understanding is 2011 is coming (have I mentioned that yet?) and that it will rest on twin pillars. One is that common people will feel an absolute compulsion to speak the plain and simple truth. The other is that as people wake up they will feel a kind of tingling process in their spines, culminating at the nape of the neck. It's just that simple. Sensei would laugh at me, I think, for not grasping that a new age will require a new, perfect language, but I am not even close to being there yet. English is a better language than I am a person so my simple idea about just speaking the truth in the language I know makes sense to me.

I'm haunted a little bit by a cartoon I saw when I was a child. A sort of nerdy-looking man was sitting next to a woman in a patent office. He had a perfectly-realized vacuum cleaner next to him. I'm old but not that old. Vacuum cleaners had already been around for a long time. She asked him: "So how long have you been up at your cabin working on your invention?" I know nothing of chakras or esoteric studies (including the Kototama Principle, which I have actually studied). One of the reasons I stopped practicing acupuncture was I had to accept the fact I didn't actually feel energy, the flow of ki. There are, I believe, enlightened or semi-enlightened people who do know these things, genuinely.

But in a way that's exactly my point. I'm not stupid, but I am basically a physical person, and I think the change that is coming will be change from the bottom up (apologies to Obama) felt like people like me or, to steal another pretty good idea, those who are last shall become first, a function, simple or not, of human consciousness as it is and the spinning of the earth through the universe.

That is the actual point of this website. If there's anything to these ideas I've been haunted by for the last year, some number of ordinary people are feeling something like I've been feeling, or will be before too long, like Homer's rosy fingers of dawn revealing the coming sunrise, and perhaps some one or two will find their way here to make a record of it.

All are welcome, of course. I've taken a stand, on twin pillars, for all time, or as long as the internet lasts and have provided space for folks here for comments and observations, condescending dismissals and rude aspersions, and even genuine tingles.

*15 November 2009*

## Well, I realize...

Well, I realize the world has waited with bated breath to learn the backstory of 12-17, the numbers. I worked with some diligence last summer to get that right—it's more of a story than I might have thought. I wrote four essays, three about the sounds, 12-17, and one called "calling shots", which was essentially about professional baseball and the possibility of seeing clearly what may be about to come.

Call it divine intervention, or good or bad luck, but then our computer simply broke (which I didn't even know computers could do) and even Apple couldn't access what was on the hard drive. It had to be somewhat unusual because they gave us a new hard drive even though our warranty had long since expired.

The point isn't what was lost but that I began to think the essays weren't all that important (except the one about calling shots—that was deep), that if the things I'm writing and feeling are true, other people can learn them for themselves if they want to, or just ask me about it. Writing it up seemed like making an argument when all I really wanted to do was make a statement or take a stand. But I have added the little essay below and I believe the comments section is now working.

*15 November 2009*

## Sustained on a...

One of the things I learned in South Dakota is that there is light in the sky before the sun actually breaks the horizon. Duh. That simple reality became a metaphor for understanding my experience of December 17th. The name of this site is sort of a playful reference to Wordsworth's poem, except the clouds of glory point to the future instead of the past.

Either it is true or it isn't that a fundamental change in human consciousness is coming. Strangely, that is not as important to me as one might think. My moment of clarity, now nearly two years ago, simply happened.

It is interesting to me that there were, so to speak, hints of that coming moment in the several years previous. That is a story in its own right, or a narrative as we say these days, but what I want to write about now is just one part of that.

On March 8, 2007, I came home from work and was lying around on the couch watching CNN when it came on the crawl that an old friend—one of the two or three best friends I made in my eight years as a professional athlete—had just died. I hadn't spoken to him in fifteen years, hadn't even known he was ill. I remember the date exactly because it was coincidentally the anniversary of my mother's sudden death from a stroke 39 years earlier.

A few days later one of my students, along with his mother, was killed in a car crash. Like anyone else in their fifties, I am not unfamiliar with death and not immune to looking in the mirror from time to time with something of a shudder. But there was just something about these two events, coming at this time of my life, in the very cold days of almost Spring (at least very cold where I live) that was almost, among many other things...disorienting.

I have always thought the most evocative adverb in all of literature comes in the dismissal of Lear by one of his two wicked daughters: "He hath ever but slenderly known himself." I stepped outside the old farmhouse where I live on one of those very cold March mornings and wrote a very short poem, the first few lines of which were:

> Who isn't Lear
> But slenderly knowing themselves
> Sustained on a fragile tendril
>         of some few words

I sent this to my sister who was kind enough to

write back and ask what the heck I was actually trying to say. I wrote her a long, rambling letter that was pretty much my philosophy of life at the time, ending with this paragraph:

> Now back to my poem with one little last note. The line that's really the heart of it is, I think obviously: "Sustained on a fragile tendril of some few words," meaning at some level our core support to continue as a human being may lie in the simplest expression of words, whose importance we ourselves may not recognize...I don't know if you know or remember anything about my old days at the Kototama Institute and the sound meditation we used to practice—but as I have said I take sound and human expression in words to be at the center of, well, everything, I guess... Somewhere along the line I have come to think of the human body as something that will finally be understood, or grasped, in terms of sound vibration. And in regard to the fragile tendril, I will just say I have been exploring the idea that the spinal column—the individual vertebrae flowing up to the brain—those vertebrae can best be under-

> stood as individual sounds. So the hidden, mysterious meaning of my poem is that the fragile tendril supporting us is that row of distinct sound vertebrae running up the spine. You might say that for me all of time and evolution and human consciousness are in that line.

This was where I was nine months or so before the night of December 17th, 2007, and in a sense it is where I still am today. That single line of poetry (and I am quite humble about my poetic abilities, if it is even poetry at all) is my philosophy of life. And my deepest understanding of what it is to be human is simply to stand on this glorious earth and make the free sounds of the Kototama Principle (admittedly slightly tweaked) with reverence and awe for the sounds themselves, the creator and the listener, and whatever level of attention we can feel for the body, especially the human spine, of the practicant.

*November 29, 2009*

## Dream

*I was a little blind girl living on a tree-lined street in Any How town and I wanted to show my friends I could fly and I took a running jump and I was flying (and I thought of my friends watching me, I wanted them to see) and I really was flying, up and farther than I could jump and I crossed the main intersection of town and was flying through the leaves of trees on the other side. Finally, I landed and was frightened and wanted more than anything, as a blind girl who now couldn't even walk, to go back home. I crawled back to the main intersection and crawled across the street without being hit and stopped at a restaurant on the right and asked the owner, who looked and acted a lot like the actor James Earl Jones, but sort of a Wizard of Oz character, in a soft gray costume, if he could help me get back home. He consulted something, a text of some kind and read me my future-- three choices. Either I could go back home, now off to the left somewhere and live forever in torment (but he at least would accompany me and live there with me) or I could do something else (I cannot remember the second option) or I could immediately confess my sins and beg forgiveness and live the rest of my life in bondage in a place further back up the road in the direction from which I had originally flown. I begged forgiveness and confessed my sins immediately, but then I hesitated there, simply didn't go, now a little further up the street but on a barren plain which now, crucially, I could see in natural light. I kneeled down and drank water from a rock, and then a voice said: "She did not stay, she did not go," over and over and I took comfort in that and then I began repeating something like: "But* (some nationality, I'm not certain—I think American) *girls do not live in fear," over and over, and I began to walk upright and without fear repeating over and over: "But American girls do not live in fear," and then saying: "And neither do Swedish girls live in fear," which made me quite happy to think about.*

Comment: This was one of those dreams for me—one of a handful I have had that are qualitatively different from the rest of my dreaming life and have carried their own import. By that I mean I don't need some outside evaluation, even my own judgment or conclusions, to validate their significance. They are more real than my waking life (well, most of it anyhow) and I find that to be validation enough.

The thing for me for this one is that for all the strangeness of it—the semi-comical nature of the James Earl Jones character and the Swedish girls, the obvious reference to a children's book (*Where the Wild Things Are*), and of course the essential oddness of dreaming myself as a little blind girl (is there a Freudian in the house?)—the most striking thing about it to me from the inside was that it was a serious, even terrifying, yet ultimately positive dream. I almost want to say cheerful. I mean this essentially in the tone or feel of it. The actual events of most of my other powerful dreams have been less frightening, but the overall impact has usually been far more ominous. This dream was so strong, so serious, and so "dreamer-friendly" in a sense that I don't even feel funny about writing "I dreamed myself as a little blind girl." Go figure.

What seems singularly important from the space of a few days later is that I was "seeing" myself as a blind girl. The street I lived on was totally black, I was blind, and yet I was functioning not only like the other kids, but as a sort of leader. I was young and athletic, as in fact I was as a child, as in fact my mother was as a child, and my wife, and my now-grown daughter. I do associate my dream self in this with those members of my family, I think most of all with my mother. Let the experts take that where they wish, but I feel this is not only because of the strong connection I feel with my now long-dead mother, but also simply because the tree-lined street was so dark and I think of the town as more like my mother's hometown in 1920's America than anywhere else.

This then takes me to what I think of as the heart of the dream—the barren plain at the end. It was quite inhospitable, except for the water I drank from a hollow in a rock, but it was *visible*, if just barely—a gray, seemingly bleak landscape but one that ultimately gave me great comfort and hope.

Now that part I can sink my teeth into. My first thought in regard to this after waking up was what I remember as almost a throwaway comment in *Black Elk Speaks* to the effect that in the real world of spirit everything is much clearer than it is to our physical eyes. Then I thought of Sensei Nakazono talking once of the experience of camping and hearing just off in the distance a continual rustling sound, of being frightened all night long, barely able to sleep, and then waking in the morning to see the sound was coming from the movement of a beautiful flower, and then Sensei concluding: "That beautiful flower is reality." It wasn't just that I had had that camping experience, in essence, but that everyone else in the class seemed to be nodding in agreement as well. And then I thought of Plato's cave. So while this barren plain was anything but a beautiful flower and was just barely visible to my eyes, it was nonetheless a glimmer of a different way of seeing.

Let me be clear. I don't want to wish myself bad luck, but I don't think I am a visionary or a seer. What Black Elk saw, for example, with great clarity, is merely the barest of outlines for me. I am barely scratching the surface here and not being sickeningly humble but just matter of fact about that. In fact, I do give myself some credit. This is the surface that I do believe all of us, or most of us, or some of us (or at least one other person, goddammit, or what an idiot I will feel like) are going to be making contact with in the very near future.

This is an important concept for me: The very black night of my dream is a metaphor for the blindness of our current state of existence which cannot see anything but physical reality. The only light in the first part of my dream, and it was a lovely, beckoning presence, was the artificial light of the restaurant on the corner. My idea now about much of the technological advancement of the past century is that the culminating effect of centuries of being afraid of the dark, and even more the metaphysical, spiritual blindness of our lives than the literal darkness, has spurred us on to physically light up the night. I thank God I have been lucky enough the last fifteen years to live in a place with no light pollution, or very little. For several years shortly after the millennium I enjoyed saying to myself as I stepped out my back door at night (as I did nearly every night, simply to see what was going on) a slightly paraphrased line from E.E. Cummings: "I step into the not merely illimitable, into the dear beautiful eternal night." I wondered about this a little. It was just a spontaneous expression for quite a long time. I think now it simply was an assertion that the natural night is where we belong.

This brings me to the first line in my dream and the name of the town, which also is a Cummings reference. My dream was not "lucid dreaming," whatever that may be, but there were things about it I seemed to know either at the time or immediately after I woke up, and the allusion to Cummings was one of them.

I'll conclude with one final observation and opinion—it is very strange from where I live just how intensely we have lit up our cities the last decade or two. I personally don't feel that fighting crime is answer enough for this phenomenon, and what I have been thinking the last few days is that the lights of our cities are a sort of Tower of Babel, trying to reach God, or spirituality, or at least fend off the darkness of our spiritual lives, purely through physical means. That didn't work out so well the last time, and I don't think it's the right way to go now either.

*15 March 2010*

## I really hate Gobekli...

Tepe. Not the archeological site itself but...it's sort of a long story.

I began studying with Sensei Nakazono in 1982. He lectured every Monday night on the Kototama Principle and over time we all became familiar with his pretty distinctive view of human history which was that an original human civilization, in the very ancient past, had discovered, not through divine intervention but through countless generations of hard work, the secrets of human existence, which happened to parallel the secrets of the existence of the universe. Yeah, it was pretty audacious.

I'm writing about it now specifically because of the time frame Sensei discussed. The original civilization peaked, as I understood his views, about 11-12 thousand years ago, and I can still see him cocking his head, as if recalculating the exact date, "about 10 thousand years ago" it was decided to hide this perfect knowledge.

I make no arguments one way or another about this view of human history. In conjunction with the rest of Sensei's teaching, to me it seemed possible, at least on a metaphorical level, for two reasons. One is there seems to be a deep wound at the very center of human existence, cross-culturally, across time, etc. But also for me personally as a young American growing up in the fifties and sixties, a young adult in the seventies—well, I think the Fugs put it best in a song—with the general sense of "Who dealt this mess?" The second reason is I thought then, and still think, in reading ancient texts that the stories from the old days about the *really* old days, the idea of a lost Golden Age, has the ring of something more than simple superstition.

Again, I am not arguing about this one way or another. I am just saying I was open to the idea. The part that makes me angry, in a calm, reasonable, detached sort of way, is I remember talking to a few people with educational backgrounds in archaeology and anthropology and so forth, mentioning my studies with Sensei Nakazono and his ideas about human pre-history. It was a hoot to them, is what I am saying, almost beyond ridicule, the idea that thousands of years before the Pyramids there was a thriving spiritual community with a very deep understanding of what was really going on.

So then Gobekli Tepe comes along in 1996, an almost unbelievable site going back 11 thousand years or more which was purposely hidden (buried) 10 thousand years ago, and which immediately, irrefutably upends all our ideas about human history and still it hasn't sunk in, it seems to me, even in the scholarly community. It reminds me of reading about a surgical procedure whose value had been pretty much discredited. The question was asked about when the procedure would be discontinued and the answer was when a new generation of surgeons had been trained in more effective methods. (And of course I'm being petty about this, but it's not like all the people that dismissed you with a horse-laugh 30 years ago call up and say, "Uh, sorry about that.")

Now I'm not saying Gobekli Tepe is validation of the Kototama Principle, or anything else. Even if underneath one of the monoliths a stone carving, unquestionably carbon-dated, in English script, is uncovered saying: "Douglas Adams was right. It's 42," undeniable proof of *something*, in other words, it's not the main thing to me. I do think, with all the anticipation of "Atlantis" emerging dramatically at some point, it's entirely possible Atlantis is rising as we speak, slowly from the Turkish desert in the form of those astonishing stone structures.

After the night of 12-17, it's funny to me that I began aligning stones in a meadow behind our house, making a row in line with the sunset at the summer solstice, for example, as closely as I could considering we live in the woods, around an old metal campfire ring we had. It's funny because I knew how silly it could be. I've been to a few sacred sites, like Chaco Canyon and the remarkable Medicine Wheel in Wyoming, and I had to laugh at the image of myself as a kind of Richard Dreyfus from *Close Encounters,* dabbling obsessively in late-middle age goofiness.

But that's as self-deprecating as I'm going to be. All those stones aligned in medicine wheels to me in one way or another are human vertebrae, which to me originally are human sounds, and I say again for me a human being is a person breathing in air down to the center at what we call tanden (a point in the lower abdomen) and speaking the sacred sounds up the channel of the spine to the brain. That's my story and I'm sticking with it.

There is something I'd missed in one of Sensei's books that I came across a couple months ago. It's from *My Past Way of Budo*, which I hadn't looked at in a long time, a line to the effect that the reason our ancestors could feel with certainty that the Kototama Principle would reemerge is that the meaning is in the sounds themselves. That is the pointn here. At the same time I am learning that ancient human history could have happened the way Sensei described, I'm also learning that the only reality of any consequence is this moment, this sound practice, this sense of wonder and gratitude for life.

*19 June 2010*

## The sky is red now and I am filled with wonder

> I don't understand why people care whether God created evolution or evolution created God. God is God. Just become like a little child and I think you will understand this.

Note: I sent this little note to the friend who helps me with this website and said I wanted it to go up at the summer solstice, along with a few final thoughts before breaking radio contact, so to speak, these last few months before "2011."

Those thoughts I've found hard to complete, but then this morning arrived like a gift from the old days, my Ohio childhood, where some summer mornings just wrapped themselves around you, around all children, I think, and felt like enough. What that feeling really is, I believe, is simply a sense of connectedness with one another and the earth and the past. And then the words that we speak to each other, the clear simple language of everyday life, reaffirm those connections. If

English is your native language and Wordsworth's poem doesn't reignite that childhood sense for you, I would suggest the Mother Goose nursery rhymes. I'm completely serious about that.

I woke up a few mornings ago with a clear understanding that our deepest connection with our human ancestors is the human voice, the sounds that we make. If you were to drop me back anywhere in time beyond a few hundred years ago, I wouldn't understand any of the words that were being spoken, or very few. But Ta is Ta. I have been thinking about these ideas of the Kototama Principle and practicing the sounds (humbly, I am anything but a monk in my daily life) for nearly 30 years, and I believe this way—"calling on the name of the lord"—is the way to search. I can't explain it any better than that. If I could give anything to another person, it would be what comes from this experience of practicing sounds over time. And the way I would describe that is simply this: More life.

*20 June 2010*

## And finally

I began attending Kototama Institute morning sound classes, led by Hikalu, in 1982. I had a cursory acquaintance with the Kototama Principle and ideas of meditation but no real idea what a "sound class" might be. I still remember my first class, at which end of the dojo I was sitting—quite a few people were in attendance that morning—things like that. Hikalu began by saying simply "Su," or "Say Su" and I knew enough to know we were supposed to make or intone that sound.

I have almost no ear for music and little knowledge of music theory, although I took piano lessons for four gloomy years as a child, a trial for my teacher as much as for me, I think. The one probably erroneous idea I got from years of practicing scales was that the first note of a musical piece was crucial—everything, the key of the song, flowing from that note. However inaccurate that may be about music, the notion that the first step is important has become almost a given for me. For example, I don't have any feel for astrology one or the other as something that might be true coming from the stars, but the idea that exactly where and when we are born on the earth is hugely important, even determinative—this seems quite reasonable to me, almost just a common-sense fact.

Long story short, my first Kototama sound, in contrast to my fellow students, most of whom had been to a class before, sounded not meditative but altogether conversational, a simple short "Su", almost as if I were speaking to my long-lost cousin of that name. It was slightly embarrassing that my short, quiet Su came to an end before my classmates, but that mild embarrassment was also a clarifying and focusing moment in a way. I have always been a little grateful also that I did not launch into a full-throated singing of the sound—not so much because that would have been embarrassing (I actually enjoy life's small humiliations. I think they build character) but because one thing it is sometimes hard to keep clear in sound practice is that it is not "singing." It is hard in our goal-oriented society not to think in terms of getting better at whatever it is we are doing, and I always thought there was a natural tendency in sound practice to think in terms of making progress, making "good sound," which is what I mean by singing. The one thing I feel pretty certain about after nearly thirty years is that it is not only, or even mainly, that you are making the sounds but also that the sounds are making you and a sense of humility about that seems important.

This was the basic format for Hikalu's sound class for the three years I attended. The class began with the repetition a few times of SU, and then SU-A-WA. Then we did the repetition of what are called the five mother and half-mother rhythms in three separate orders (the names of the orders are Sugaso, Kanagi, and Futonolito). That would be A O U E I WA WO WU WE WI. Then A I U E O WA WI WU WE WO. And then A I E O U WA WI WE WO WU. And then I can still hear Hikalu saying, first "5 free sounds. Then "5-7-5." Then "5-7-5 7-7." That last pattern, like a Japanese tanka, we would repeat numerous times. It is the basic form for making what are called free sounds. Finally we would end with the repetition of the 50 sounds in Futonolito order. There were a few other elements to the sound practice that we did on occasion, but I believe these things we did every time.

Probably the two best questions I asked Sensei in my time at the Kototama Institute were, first: On the human body, are the Yu points the mother sounds and the Bo points the half-mother sounds? Then later before an internship class I asked again about the Yu points and Bo points and also if the other eight important points located on the extremities might be related to the eight father rhythms of the Kototama Principle. I say these were the two best questions because of Sensei's reaction to this one. He said this was something he was still exploring himself.

Not surprisingly, I never got anywhere with that, but it did encourage me to keep thinking of the human body and the sounds of the Kototama Principle. The configuration of the vertebrae on the human spine was always interesting to me—I don't see how it couldn't be to any practitioner. We frequently used the back Yu points in internship practice and I carried that into my own practice. Locating points on the spine, the feel of the change from thoracic to lumbar vertebrae—it seemed important to me, and just the fact of twelve thoracic vertebrae seemed especially important. I always thought for a couple of reasons these divided naturally below T-5 into what are called the upper and middle heat. Then there are seven cervical and five lumbar vertebrae. And then the five sacral vertebrae which I know western medicine views as one fused bone, but still we located points in practice as below S-1 and S-2. (And I do know also about the sacrum, thereby hangs another tale.) Eventually, I began thinking about the similarity between the spine and the pattern of free sounds, the relatively small difference, and also thinking about the hidden aspects of the Kototama Principle, the idea that the old knowledge had been intentionally covered over, and simply wondered might there be anything in some pattern of free sounds based not on 31 but on 29. I literally thought about this for years until, in a spirit of humility, I began to investigate combinations of 5-7-5-7-5 with some level of attention in practice to the spine. Coincidence or not, I began to feel the most interesting kind of tingling sensation along the spine culminating very clearly with a strong sensation at the base of the neck.

This explains about as well as I can the 5-7 5-5-7 jolt after my experience on Dec. 17th. It is, to me, coincidence and irony but also so far a seemingly endless source for meditation. I certainly make no claims about it outside my own experience. It was pretty interesting to me to read somewhere in the last few weeks that a couple of scientists are claiming to have found a hidden message in the Sistine Ceiling painting. Through some sort of spectroscopic analysis, I believe, they have concluded that Michelangelo included a hidden representation of human vertebrae, the spinal column, leading up to the vocal cords of God. Nearly always, it seems to me, these kinds of findings turn out not to be true or quite a bit different from the way they are first reported. But if by chance this is true, I just want to say I really agree with Michelangelo on that one—which is a very fun thing to write down.

I want to conclude with a note about Hikalu himself. I wish I could capture the dignity and gravitas and humility he brought to sound class. I never knew a great deal about his past, but he was of European Jewish descent and in his sixties when I first met him in the early 1980's. He had suffered a stroke sometime earlier, was physically frail, and one of his hands shook. I remember a number of simple, specific things he said. Sometimes I think the best way to remember people is simply to collect whatever it is they said that we can remember exactly, word for word, but that is not what I want to do here. I will say that once, in the middle of sound class, out of the blue, so to speak—it was unusual in my recollection for Hikalu to speak on any topic during the sound meditation itself—he made the most prescient comment about Israel.

I played baseball briefly in the big leagues thirty years ago and one of the cities I played in as a member of a visiting team was New York. We stayed in midtown Manhattan. I was like a child in a candy store when I visited Manhattan in those days, staring up at the skyscrapers, racing through as many rooms as I could at the Metropolitan Museum of Art in an hour or two, and so forth. *Apocalypse Now* premiered at the movie theater across the street from my hotel during this stay. Eddie Condon's jazz club was half a block away.

One afternoon I took the train by myself to Shea Stadium for that night's game. Just riding on a train in New York was an adventure for me in those days. I probably thought I looked like Roy Scheider in *The French Connection*, holding onto an arm strap, checking out the scene. I remember it was very sunny as we rose up on whatever bridge it would have been to cross whatever river you cross to get from mid-town to the ball park when I noticed the old man seated directly below me was reading a foreign-language newspaper. I am a compulsive reader, whether I know the language or not, and in this case I stared long enough and knew enough to figure out it was in Hebrew. Then I noticed the old man had a number tattooed on his forearm. I am not an impolite person and not one to stare, but I guess I looked at that tattoo for as long as I wanted to. I think I realized even at that moment it was a concentration-camp tattoo, but it was quite some time before I learned that only at Auschwitz were inmates given number tattoos. And it is only recently, after rereading Elie Wiesel's *Night* (just as a school assignment, really—I had a group of freshman I was giving independent reading time to in class and I wanted to read along with them, be a role model) but it is only recently, I say, that I have realized that old man must have been intensely aware of me looking down, peering down, at him and that his awareness connected him in that moment, and me, to that previous horror. I am of European descent also, although not Jewish, and I was 26 years old then and a large person and very fit—young and strong—and altogether ignorant.

I have written already about what I have called Hikalu's eternal "Ta!" and I meant it—the sound of it will stay with me, I think, for as long as I live. But it is only recently also, sitting out in my Midwestern garage on summer evenings, that I have really meditated on it. I don't know how much can be held in one syllable. I have heard Elie Wiesel say, just in a television interview, that every word we say about the Holocaust must be a sacred word. I agree with that, but then I would also add that every word we say about the Middle Passage, and every word we say about the decimation of America from a Native American point of view, should be similarly serious. And then it just keeps going for me, all the way down to Salinger's Fat Lady (not Yogi Berra's, this one is different, but her too, I suppose) and finally to all sentient beings, every word that we speak about everything. I really agree with Jesus on that one. Ta is Ta, I have also written earlier, but you should have heard Hikalu's "Ta!" —holding in a sacred way, I believe, such a part of the twentieth century.

That's how I feel about Hikalu.

*8 August 2010*

## Coda: When I was a child...

When I was a child I occasionally had the most terrifying feeling. It was similar to the sensation I think many of us have felt waking up at an odd time or in an unfamiliar place and not being quite sure just who we are. That sensation to me is not altogether unpleasant and one I feel that I can take control of rather simply. This other feeling was something different—a profound awareness that my deepest sense of me was no different from the way every other living creature feels about its own existence. Describing it this way—as clearly as I can—it doesn't seem to be something that should be so frightening. In fact, on the face of it, it would seem to describe the Sense of Oneness with All Things that is supposed to bring great peace and understanding. But it *was* most frightening—a consciousness that totally obliterated any meaning to my distinctive consciousness and individual existence. There are, I believe, a million ways that we learn to fear death, but this feeling became the bedrock for me of what I would call a really robust level of death anxiety.

I don't think that this sensation is unique to me, but I have only read or heard it described one other time. Probably twenty years ago, *The New Yorker* carried a profile of an up-and-coming conductor of classical music. He was apparently a huge talent and an interesting personality, and I remember an enigmatic paragraph where he described exactly in a few words this feeling I am writing about. He found it to be a terrifying experience also.

I think the mentality of our current civilization today is to pit our individual existence and consciousness literally against all the rest of time and the universe. The futility of this point of view is what my childhood moments revealed to me—at least that is the way I look at it now. The truly final point I want to make on this website is that I believe the Kototama Principle is the way to bridge the seemingly unbridgeable gap between our individual consciousness and eternity. Human expression in words, or sounds, is the universe, not just metaphorically but in actual fact. Our bodies and the way that we speak are composed of the same elements as time and matter. Grasping this, I believe, is the fundamental thing that human beings should do. It doesn't negate the fact of death (Darnit!) but, it is at the very least a profound comfort.

*February 17, 2011*

## Notes on 2011

This was a heady time for me. I thought the Arab Spring, unfolding so dramatically, in the shadow of the pyramids...words fail. I made the following four posts on this day in February. The first three were things I'd been thinking about for a while. The last very brief one will follow with an explanation. I joked in June of 2010 about breaking off radio silence before re-emerging in 2011. Between the Arab Spring and the way I was feeling on the 17th, these posts actually did feel a little like landing safely in a new place, one I had been looking for.

*On Intimations*

These are the relevant passages from the William Wordsworth poem I referred to a couple times earlier and which inspired the title of this website. One of the best students I ever had is familiar with the writing here and wasn't familiar with this poem, so I have decided to include it with a few comments below.

## Intimations of Immortality
## from Recollections of Early Childhood

### I

There was a time when every meadow, grove, and stream
The earth and every common sight,
To me did seem
Appareled in celestial light,
The glory and the freshness of a dream
It is not now as it hath been of yore, —
Turn wheresoe'er I may,
By night or day,
The things which I have seen I now can see no more.

### V

Our birth is but a sleep and a forgetting.
The Soul that rises with us, our life's star
Hath had elsewhere its setting,
And cometh from afar.
Not in entire forgetfulness and not in utter nakedness
But trailing clouds of glory do we come
From God, who is our home.
Heaven lies about us in our infancy!

Shades of the prison-house begin to close
Upon the growing Boy
But he beholds the light, and whence it
flows
He sees it in his joy,
The Youth, who daily farther from the east
Must travel, still is Nature's priest,
And by the vision splendid
Is on his way attended.
At length the Man perceives it die away,
And fade into the light of common day.

— William Wordsworth

I first encountered this in high school and then later in a couple of college literature classes. I came back to it from time to time over the years, realizing at some point it resonated so deeply for me because I felt someone was finally describing, far better than I ever could, what it is really like to be a child. That fading of an ineffable glory was almost palpable for me. There were snapshots of existence I carried around in my head as a record of that different level of reality, and I felt quite clearly and thought about, when I was in grade school, that ability fading.

It was almost funny how much I disliked some of the children's books then—*The Cat in the Hat* in particular. Thing One and Thing Two were like my worst nightmares—adult used-car salesmen with hideous combovers shrunk down to mini-little whirlwinds of entropy and chaos.

There's a paragraph from Peter Matthiessen, taken from *The Snow Leopard*, writing about his infant son at play, which also captures this childhood sense, at least for me. I have read that passage along with the excerpt from "Intimations of Immortality" nearly every year with students and tried to discuss, without beating it to death, whether or not they still have that kind of feeling about childhood. Many do.

*I'm not saying,*

I'm just saying...

I was serious on this site when I wrote that one part of what "2011" would mean is that common people would feel an absolute compulsion to tell the plain and simple truth. I understand the tendency and even the need to create a narrative about what has happened and will happen in Egypt. Personally, I credit the Pyramids. Just kidding, but to me this certainly seems to be people having an inner sense of truth that just can't be bottled up any longer.

Somebody else reports that old tingling sensation in the neck I also wrote about and I'm going to claim victory, spike one in the end zone, and retire to my garden in the back meadow.

*Old Ballplayer*

This poem I wrote in the early days of what I now think of as a process leading up to night of December 17, 2007. I was 54 in the winter of 2006. Most interesting to me is the "sense of fitness" description and the "bow your neck" line. I don't think I know a lot about the sound practice except just to do it, in the way I was taught and have already described. I do think some sort of breathing exercise focused on quietude and breathing down to tanden, a point on the lower abdomen, is most helpful, perhaps even necessary. And I have become pretty particular about posture during sound practice. The heart of that for me is just about as simple as "bow your neck"—a feeling of chin down instead of chin up, so to speak.

## *On an Old Ballplayer Getting Back in Shape*

Fifty-four years old—two cups of coffee in the
big leagues
eight full seasons in the minors
no regrets about any of it

and a lot has happened since
for ten years an acupuncturist
a schoolteacher for twelve
a family man, a grower of natural food

in one of those minor-league off seasons
I watched the sun set from my back porch in
Santa Fe,
transfixed, "sealed in eternity" as I put it once
in a poem*

and on one of those nights
I stepped off the deck and walked
down among the pinon trees, and I was sur-
prised,
bowled over, to feel inside myself,
deeply, just how much I loved to play ball,
the whole life—and how much I would miss
it
if it ever ended

now on a frozen December morning that selfsame sun
rises over my old, cold northern Michigan farmhouse
where after several years I have begun working out again

and I sit in the still dark morning with a fresh cup of coffee,
a fire just started in our ancient woodstove
(inefficient like me, but brother it puts out the heat)
and the only thing I feel is the resonance of last night's workout—
deep down the old familiar feeling of a body in shape—
the tightness in the abdomen and the corresponding sense
of fitness in the neck and shoulders

"Bow your neck!" we used to shout out at each other
in the 70's by way of encouragement
and none of us, I think, knew quite what that meant
but everyone understood the sense of preparedness it conveyed

perhaps now for me, approaching old age
    and death,
that simple sense of fitness is all there is,
and I just may go gently into that dark
    night after all,
gently and flexibly, with a core of light and
    strength ,
humble as it may be

and who knows? perhaps from that kernel,
"immortal diamond", that simple sense of
    readiness,
stripped of all identity

will spring

a new genesis

*This is the full text of that song for the setting sun

Santa Fe, 1978

Lonesome Dog's Barking
*All my fantasies are realized*
*I have a view of Santa Fe from my back porch*
*That just won't quit*

*tonight I saw the pinkest thin vein of cloud as the sun set*
*whether I was the only one to feel it or not*
*it seals me in eternity*

*There is only the wind*
*Whistling through the mountaintops*
*Of this world*

***Lord have mercy***

*on me, a sinner*

I woke up early on this morning of Feb. 17, 2011. I had been eating well, working out, generally taking care of myself. As I said earlier, this physical plane of existence is one I feel deeply, am quite at home with, and this particular morning I just felt really good. But more than that was this sound practice feeling, this tingling all along the spine—just really and most intensely, another term I also earlier: More Life. I just felt so powerfully what we are capable of as human beings, what I had been capable of all along, and I felt especially how far short I had fallen of that, all along the way. In short, it was the beauty and the pain, and I never felt so sincerely a prayer as I did this one on this day.

*17 December 2011*

## Poem for Mohamed Bouazizi

*palimpsest*

There is a meadow
and in the background
are all the books ever written,
all the ancestors,
every moment of beauty and pain
in the history of the universe

In the foreground
there is just the meadow,
a human being,
the sound practice

## An Atheist No More

When you are 60 years old and
Have been splitting wood for heat
the last 30,
Go outside during a January thaw,
Find an old pine stump
You didn't split last spring,
Some old pine that lived heroically
And stoically, long ago in the wind,
Now just a last stump long-dead,
Raise your maul up to the sky
And split that stump in a warm January
breeze,
Lift an old dead split pine shard
Up to your face and breathe deep

And then tell me there isn't a god

There are a few reasons I think this may actually be a poem, but the most important to me is that, almost immediately, I realized what had just come to me spontaneously was also a perfect symbolic representation of my whole life—the sound practice, taking these heroic but dead words from the old days, my first 30 years, splitting them open and then with all my physical and spiritual senses, if only for a moment, breathing deep and grasping their total heart.

In that spirit, after 30 years, I am announcing that I will be conducting my first Kototama sound class, in the style of Hikalu, open to anyone that is interested. It will be held on August 9, on top of Thunder Butte in South Dakota, sometime in mid-morning. There will be a meet-up at the diner in Isabel at 8:00 a.m. I'm pretty sure there's just one place there that counts as a sit-down restaurant, but in the event of any confusion, I will be at the place that has a vehicle with Michigan plates parked outside. Trust me, it won't be hard for us to find each other. It's about a five-hour hike to the top of the butte and back with time enough for a sound meditation included.

Cost: well, breakfast is on me. Other than that, you're on your own. I will say that later that evening I plan to attend the opening of the Rock Creek

Powwow an hour or so away. If anyone wants to go to that as well, dinner will be my treat too.

I want to say a few words about that powwow. I stumbled on it the first year (2008). I went out to South Dakota and have returned for portions of the three-day event every year since. I am strictly a visitor, claim no understanding or connection with the culture, but will say just being there does my heart good somehow.

I remember asking one of the instructors at the Kototama Institute if the Revolution (I was referring to Sensei's ideas about 2011, but this was 1982 and something of the 60's was still in the air) was going to be urban or rural. I still wonder about that. In fact, the question seems even more urgent now if we understand urban to mean technology and rural to mean the natural life. I don't presume to know, and I mainly just hope for better days ahead for human beings and the human spirit. But it's a late spring this year where I am, and as I am typing this, I occasionally look out the window at the field out back and think of the billions of seeds and eggs in that one field that are on the absolute verge of exploding into life.

I understand a little, I think, about the intoxication of this astonishing new technological age, and big data, and the storage capacity of microchips.

But it seems to me that each microscopic seed in my backyard is storing a connection going back to the origins of life, ultimately to the beginning of time, and contains information that can sustain life forward for probably a finite but potentially an infinite future. This seems a little more miraculous to me than even the most amazing of possible future cyber-existences. Actually, a lot more miraculous.

What I am saying is, I will take my chances with the natural way. And if indeed this present moment is a turning point in human history (as every moment must certainly be, but let's face it: the stakes are pretty high for the human race these days) a guy could do worse than attend the Rock Creek Wacipi and find a center for changing the world at the center of that powwow circle, where even to a stranger like me, it is clear the people feel that the earth is sacred, and that human beings have a sacred responsibility to it, and to each other.

*18 July 2014*

## Second verse...

...same as the first, except even quieter. I'll be at the diner in Isabel Monday morning, August 11, at 8 o'clock for breakfast and then a hike to the top of Thunder Butte should anyone wish to go. Last year aside from an open invitation to the world I personally contacted or invited roughly a couple dozen people. Three met me there. But this August will be a quiet one for me on the Plains, poking around and thinking things over. This year's ruminations on the Kototama sound practice below.

Harold Bloom has written, as I am able to understand him, that Shakespeare changed the world, or human consciousness, because his characters changed through "overhearing" themselves speak. It occurs to me that this is pretty much exactly what happens in Kototama sound practice except one overhears the basic sounds of the human voice without the arbitrary meanings assigned by one or another particular human language. The audacity of the Kototama Principle, I believe, is to assert not just that these sounds have meaning in themselves, but that they are the fundamental building blocks of reality.

For a long time, my understanding was that one part, perhaps the biggest part, of human beings waking up was to begin to speak in daily life a sort of one true Kototama language. That is, there is one right word for everything and if we speak it out—if we look at the mountain and call it by its true name—we will inevitably come into harmony with things, and this will be the New Age for the human race.

That may be so, but as I wrote on my original post on this site five years, I am not even close to being there yet. In fact, it is more interesting to me now to consider that there may be two kinds of language for human beings, the sound meditation and the language of daily life.

The first way I want to discuss this idea of dual languages is to refer to bicameralism—the ideas of Julian Jaynes. Now I don't want to give the wrong idea here; basically all I know of Jaynes' ideas is what I've read in the occasional essay that pops up from time to time on *3 Quarks Daily* or *Arts and Letters*. But it seems almost too perfectly related to the Kototama Principle, the history of it as Sensei Nakazono used to present it. The idea seems to be the ancients were incapable of introspective thought, but instead, were guided by voices in their heads that they took to be the voices of the gods. My understanding is that in Jaynes' view then there was a kind of evolution into modern-day capacity for inwardness or introspection, a big step up from the strangeness of ancient awareness.

This idea makes a Kototama person sit up and take notice—or at least it is intriguing to me—but from a Kototama perspective the idea would be that the old "voices of the gods" is the sound meditation language still echoing in the ears, you might say, of the human race even though the practice itself had been stopped. In other words, after we stopped making the sounds of Kototama, we eventually lost our ears, our ability to hear those sounds, which near the end seemed as strange and mysterious as the voices of the gods.

(You can test this out for yourself. Take the basic sounds of Sugaso order—I A O U E—pronouncing the I as in be and the E as in way, say them three times quickly and then go look in the mirror and say Candym...just kidding.)

Richard Dawkins, as I recall, has described Jaynes' work as either complete rubbish or something wonderful. So is the writing on this website, but I am beginning to think, or at least get glimpses, that from the sound practice emerges a second kind of consciousness that is quite outside the confines of my everyday language. I am not quite sure what to make of that last sentence. I am trying to grow some new ears is basically what I believe I am saying.

This spring I read Robert Utley's biography of Sitting Bull and came across this very striking paragraph from a letter sent by ten Hunkpapa chiefs in 1862 to Pierre Garreau at Fort Berthold, dealing essentially, it seems to me, with the heart of a conflict between two very different cultures:

> "We notified the Bear's Rib yearly not to receive your goods; he had no ears and we gave him ears by killing him. We now say to you, bring us no more goods; if any of our people receive any more from you we will give them ears by killing them as we did the Bear's Rib...We have told all our agents the same thing, but they have paid no attention to what we have said. If you have no ears, we will give you ears, and then your father likely will not send us any more goods or agent.
>
> We also say to you that we want you to stop the whites from travelling through our country, and if you do not stop them,

> we will. If your whites have no ears, we will give them ears."

This affected me at first, almost viscerally, just as an old athlete. Odd as this may sound, it seemed like the best kind of trash talking, bold and threatening but also intensely serious, honest, and confident. Then the sadness of it—first that they were aware the strange powers approaching were deaf to their voices, and then the historical knowledge we have that the deaf ones had the power and were going to use it mercilessly.

And then finally the surprising and incredibly eloquent connection with my own Christian upbringing—how well I remember Jesus saying: "He who has ears, let him hear." I believe we all think we understand this saying, and we all believe that we are the ones in the know, that we have the right kind of ears. So why after 2000 years of Christian ascendancy is the world still so screwed up?

Jesus also said that we all must become like little children, and I believe I understood that in the way he meant it. In fact, it runs pretty deep in me. The title of this website is a salute to Wordsworth's powerful visualization of this, and I always thought the disciples were being either incredibly dense or willfully obtuse with—so what are you saying, we have to go back in the womb? It never occurred to me, though, to wish that someone had said: "So where can a guy get a pair of those ears?" Or that Jesus had just outlined that quite specifically. Well, and I hope it's obvious by now, my idea about the way to grow the right kind of ears is to overhear yourself—for me it works best out in a meadow somewhere—in Kototama sound practice.

One last thing, "Intimations of Immortality" begins with the line: "The child is father of the man." Perhaps my favorite English poet, Gerard Manley Hopkins, has a short poem dismissing this as nonsense, but I always thought it made perfect sense. I've asked young students about it several times over the years and they've pretty much come up empty, which doesn't happen too often.

I've also asked young people if our ancestors are younger or older than us, are they the ancient ones or the young ones, and this has been an interesting thing to talk about with them.

Related to this, but harder for me to get a handle on, is what I think should be the relatively simple idea of "foreground". Emerson famously speculated on the foreground of Walt Whitman's poetry. And again, about Harold Bloom, when I first taught a high school class on Shakespeare ten years ago, I can't tell you how many times I read and reread his discussion of foregrounding and Shakespeare. I just couldn't see it until one day I was walking out to the meadow behind our house and got the little poem included here earlier.

What I'm getting to is, it seems to me now that being born is not just a "coming into" but also a "coming from". The language of everyday life is the language of coming into awareness and knowledge, individuation, and so forth. But the language of the sound practice, which we have lost, is the language of connection—and I've tried pretty hard to avoid this kind of sweeping statement—connection with the universe from which we have come, of which we are a part, and to which we will return.

I reread Black Elk's great vision this year pretty closely, for the first time in quite a while. I was particularly taken with the voice "that went all over the universe and filled it". I believe we all know what this is. It's in the Bible, particularly I think in Psalms, it's in Abraham Lincoln's pretty remarkable "mystic chords of memory" line—hell, to me it is even in a sports stadium rocked by cheers for what people are watching unfold in front of their very eyes.

My story once again, which I continue to stick with, is that this Kototama Principle of sound meditation is the way to access this connection, to join the poet in saying: “now the ears of my ears awake and now the eyes of my eyes are opened.”

*17 December 2014*

## Sound Practice

I am including here a link to a tape I made of myself doing the sound practice with some small commentary. It's homemade and amateurish—quite appropriate in a way, and I am not taking a shot at myself saying that. One of the things Hikalu said to me about sound class and the sound practice was: "You have to be desperate." In this case, that applies pretty much to my attempts to get the word out about the Kototama Principle and to any person who might stumble on my efforts and be moved to action by them. Mainly I just sort of felt like an athlete about it. This is what I have been talking about, which seems only fair to put out there, and this is the way I did it on October 25, 2014.

One of the hard things about this Kototama Principle, I think, is that talking about it in everyday language is doomed to failure. One reason I made the tape is the Kototama videos I have seen on YouTube sound so much like chanting, something quite apart from "normal" human sounds. Mine may as well, but my sense after all these years is that the sound practice is simply more real or normal than everyday language. It is the perspective from which everyday language is created.

I still feel I know next to nothing about the actual sounds. I have to smile about sort of choking up at one point saying: "A - I - E." Those three sounds, the heart as I understand it, of the final basic order, do in fact give me pleasure somehow, perhaps will be my final prayer if I am allowed one. I could go on and on about that. Those three sounds represent respectively light, life-will, and judgment, have a certain primacy over O and U, representing knowledge and the physical desires and reality. Or I could relate them to the human body—the "human form divine" as William Blake puts it—head and broad shoulders and chest tapering down to a narrow waist and skinny legs. Or even a buffalo's body. You don't have to shout: "Bow your neck!" to a buffalo, words which, as I have written elsewhere here, sort of capture my sense of posture during sound practice. Sit a buffalo upright and you would be pretty much good to go. But these are just ideas. The sound practice itself is the thing.

And finally a note about, of all things, the poet Gerard Manley Hopkins. I have loved his poetry since first encountering it in college. I have recited to myself and classes of students, for instance, "Spring and Fall" countless times over the last 40 years, and it still gives me both pleasure and pain. Frankly I also always liked that he didn't write so much. I've come to the conclusion that most writers, or at least most "serious" ones, write too much. Elmore Leonard's idea that a prospective writer needs to write 100,000 words to find his or her voice makes sense to me, but after that there's only so many bullets in the gun, as a pretty good major-league pitcher said to me once.

But in regard to the Kototama Principle, there is the sound A. Only recently have I realized that a basic appeal of Hopkins' poetry for me has always been his use of "Ah" as a kind of interjection. In "Spring and Fall" it is: "Ah, as the heart grows older". Most striking to me is this:

> "Oh, morning, at the brown brink eastward, springs
> Because the Holy Ghost over the bent
> World broods with warm breast and with ah! bright wings"

And in perhaps his greatest poem:

> "No wonder of it: sheer plod makes plow down sillion
> Shine, and blue-bleak embers, ah my dear,
> Fall, gall themselves, and gash gold-vermillion"

What I am saying is there a splendor breaking from Hopkins' poetry, at least to my ears, in the repetition of that single syllable a handful of times that is unique in English poetry and distinctly Kototama-like in spirit.

Here's the link:
https://www.youtube.com/watch?v=Z72O9s-NhG0

## Notes

There is here, after the "Sound Practice" post on 17 December 2014, a six-year hiatus on any writing appearing on my hidden, super-secret, mysterious-prophetic website *Intimations of 2011*. Up to this point, all the writing in Part 2 of this book, Out of My Life and..., just followed naturally, to me at least, from the first, or home-page essay. I use the phrase "And finally" more than once, I believe, or words to that effect, because the content of each new post just sort of arrived for me, and related to that initial post, and was generally what I thought would be my last words on the matter.

So now this six-year break which I am writing about here from the vantage point of 2023.

There were basically three things going on. One is I just didn't have anything to write about relating to all this for the next couple years, and I basically wasn't interested in writing about anything else. My entire literary output for 2015, for example, was one haiku:

If you want to be
consider the seasons and
dwell in the words

And I was pretty much ok with this, as what I had to say for that year, except it was a little irritating, considering the amount of time I spent in meditative posture making sounds, sacred sounds I believed, and still do, in patterns of 5-7-5, was more than a little irritating that I couldn't get the number of syllables right in that last line.

The next year all of my writing added up to 8 haikus, one of which was the one for my mother included here earlier. And again, I was ok with this. In fact I looked at it, if at all critically, as quite an acceptable level of progress, thinking if I continued at that rate and lived long enough, I might wind up making a pretty good statement about this life, from my point of view, in haiku form.

But there were a couple other things going on in this time period. In 2017, I got a poem which I felt led me to the brink of writing a new post about all the website matters—the Kototama Principle, the state of the world and so forth. But early in 2017, and for the next couple years, I experienced a couple pretty serious health issues. The post I wanted to write—it was really quite important to me, starting as I said from a poem—was the way I had come to view the sound practice as prayer, and the way I had come to understand prayer itself over the years.

I can prove, sort of, I had this post or essay in nascent form back then. The health things began with a fairly dramatic experience early in 2017 with me winding up in hospital with tubes protruding from orifices I don't care to discuss. I only mention this because, in the fairly early moments of the crisis, when my wife first visited me in a hospital room, I asked her to write down the basic form of these things I'd been thinking. I don't want to overstate the crisis—I don't think there was much chance, if any, of imminent death. But still, the point is it was that important to me.

I did try more than once to finish that essay and, no excuses, I just couldn't. The next year I had a separate health situation, mentioned again here earlier in a poem. I do think in retrospect I just couldn't get the right kind of energy together to complete those thoughts or that piece of writing. But the importance of it has remained for me, and I finally write about it at the end of the book.

The third reason I believe I posted nothing on the website for so many years is increasingly I was exploring the things my vision (or "vision", as I still feel compelled to say) led me to discover in South Dakota, most specifically Lakota culture.

There is a great void-space in the center of the record of my second vision—the essay beginning this portion of the book. It comes between watching the sunrise at Sitting Bull's grave three mornings in a row, trying to write about why I was there in the first place, and then the experience on the road on the way home. In the middle was me stumbling on the Rock Creek V-J Day Celebration, which was an overwhelming experience for me. I felt pretty much compelled to return for the next several years, never mentioning the experience here until 2013.

So, in that period roughly from 2014 to 2020, the second basic conclusion was beginning to take shape. The first, coming from the Donnie Moore vision and essay was that we simply don't understand, grasp, or fully acknowledge the depths of our collective racism, the power of it, both blatant and insidious.

The second is there is something in Lakota culture the world needs, and this became a matter of increasing interest and importance to me. I rather doubt I'm the one to make the determination about what that is, although, after quite a few years I am willing to make a statement about it. There are certain specific possibilities that people there have talked about with me a little—particularly the chanupa (pipe) and the ceremonies.

There is a third one also discussed and you'll probably be shocked to discover it is the one I have come to favor: the language.

More about this—the story of making greater contact with Lakota people and culture—also comes later in the book. I will only say that for a long time now my favorite story about a holy person experiencing something that we take to be outside the possibilities of actual human experience, and also which I feel most certain actually happened, is the story of Sitting Bull walking out on the prairie one morning at sunrise shortly before his death and a bird saying to him: "A Lakota will kill you."

In 2021, I wound up talking one day in Bullhead with Courtney Brown Otter about why I had been coming out there all these years. At one point I mentioned this Sitting Bull story (we were only a few miles from the spot on the Grand River where Sitting Bull was killed) and Courtney said to me that the meadowlarks speak Lakota.

I talked last summer with Jerry Dearly, a popular longtime Lakota powwow emcee. Basically, I'm a big fan of his. I felt as early as 15 years ago that he was a national treasure that the nation unfortunately didn't know about. When we talked, I asked if he had spoken Lakota growing up. He said the squirrels spoke Lakota; their dogs spoke Lakota.

*25 February 2020*

## 2020: A Kototama Manifesto

*early morning poem*

It has taken me a long time
But I am no longer in dialogue
With the world
Now there is just this piece
Of paper and the true words
I have written, linking me
To the true words I have heard
And spoken, linking me
To the sights and sounds
Of the true world—
Birdsong and sunrise
Sunset and evening song

There is a spectre haunting the universe. It is the spectre of birdsong and the Kototama sound practice.

The unified theory of everything is human consciousness and the human voice. This vanishing neutrino of a single human life is capable of grasping in an instant the life of the stars and the universe and eternity, and this happens at the minutest cellular, even sub-atomic, level inside one's own skull. It is almost as if (almost!) who needs eternal life?

The birds sing this daily, and the poets know it too:

> To see a World in a Grain of Sand
> And a Heaven in a Wildflower,
> Hold Infinity in the palm of your hand
> And Eternity in an hour
> —William Blake

And:

> I'd rather learn from one bird how to sing
> Than teach 10,000 stars how not to dance
> —E.E. Cummings

Even the physicists are in on it:

> "It was not possible to formulate the laws of quantum mechanics in a fully consistent way without reference to human consciousness".
> —E. Wigner

And finally, it is interesting to me in my old age that the best summation of the human condition should come from Isaiah: All flesh is grass, but the Word endures forever.

I rest my case.

## Tanka: To 2021—Kototama Sound Practice

Sitting in seiza
the curvature of the spine
brother or sister

to the curvature of the
world—a new globe at the top

*22 September 2021*

## 2021: Part 2

"Until you have cried for the fate of every sentient being, you cannot be a real human being"

*(There is a through-line in all my writing, from childhood feelings to visions, dreams, poems, experience, prayer—everything, winding up on the back road from Bullhead to Isabel, just above the Grand River, a few miles west of Sitting Bull's camp.)*

In July, I made the drive one early evening from Bullhead to Isabel, the first 15 miles on a good dirt road, hardly travelled on, and beautiful. It had been a good day, almost a great day, making plans for this venture I've cared about so much, sharing with another person there my grandmother dream, seemingly making good practical things happen, the sun setting in front of me, a favorite song playing, me speeding up as the music kicks in, and goddammit if a meadowlark doesn't rise up in front of me, and I hear the thump.

This is not a new thing. I know this is meadowlark country. I know they are slow to avoid the cars compared to the other birds, almost as if the beauty of their voices and their bodies is some kind of weight, a price they pay. I went out to check and of course it is there, but not dead—yet—only broken, with its head up, alert.

I pick it up and carry it to the side of the road and I am heartbroken and wildly hypocritical, feeling this hypocrisy as I weep and place it gently in the grass, apologizing (fucking hypocrite!), speaking out loud, profoundly conscious of this holy landscape all around, of the proximity to Sitting Bull's camp, where one morning at sunrise a meadowlark said to him: "A Lakota will kill you."

Then the meadowlark, broken and crippled, did the most astonishing thing: It flew, or attempted to, achieving a kind of lift-off before flipping over completely and landing helplessly, failing (and Dylan Thomas's words, which I have railed against, were right there: Do not go gentle). And I felt the soul leave its body. Then the meadowlark, with indescribable dignity, its lower body completely paralyzed, raised its head and cleaned, preened the underside of the wing it could reach, and then laid down its head and...accepted. And I felt its body go back in the earth, its eyes closing slowly, the light going out (no fear or regret—O my soul!). Then with eyes halfway closed, an ant crawled directly onto one of them, almost as if to suck the last little light of life out for itself, it seemed to me, and I said: "Not on my watch" and brushed it aside, wondering if it really was what it seemed, and the ant crawled back once more, brushed aside once more, and then the meadowlark was gone.

## Coincidence

On Oct. 19:

I cleaned out a drawer, filled with papers,
And burned all those sins
This morning, I found this
Crumpled note on the basement floor,
Next to the woodstove,
The sole survivor:

"John 90 AD
The Word became flesh
John (Me) 2018
The flesh became Word

I don't understand why people care
whether God created evolution
Or evolution created God

The holy spirit is breath entering the body
And the breath leaving the body is sound, a
holy sound"

Now with the World in flames
This tattered flesh hangs
By a thread,
A scrap of paper
A single breath,
A coincidence,
And a holy sound

(Note: Perhaps it seems overly dramatic, but I really was in despair at this point over ... the upcoming non-presidential election, with the predictions of a Red Wave, just two years after Trump's defeat, not even two years after January 6.)

*22 September 2023*

## 3 Verdicts

When God is pulling together all the
strands of the universe,
mixing with the DNA at hand to create a
new human being,
there is a moment s/he can see everything
that will happen
in this new life, how every decision and
concatenation of
circumstance and coincidence will actually
play out,
and in a voice that fills the whole universe
for a moment
God speaks, with infinite gradations of
irony and meaning,
one of three verdicts:
"Man, that's progress!"
or
"If the fool would persist in his folly, he
would become wise"
or
"That's fucked up, man!"

This is exhausting work and God then falls
asleep,
awaking refreshed, remembering,
imagining
that human's future as a kind of dream,
which like human dreams quickly fades,
and the human plays out his destiny alone
and this is why when we are born
we cry that we are come into this world
of so much beauty and pain

My summer road trips out to Standing Rock were usually planned pretty far in advance, but in May of 2023 it felt pretty good for once to just jump in my car and head west. Reminded me of the old days and a baseball story and I sent this note to my kids the morning of departure:

> In 1980 a Philadelphia sportswriter wrote a column at the end of spring training about guys sent back to the minor leagues, and included a part about me heading out to OKC in my '70 Pinto with 100,000 miles on it. Now in 2023 I'm heading out to SD in my 2009 KIA with 200,00 miles on it. Man, that's progress!
> love,
> dad

The sportswriter was Frank Dolson, with the *Philadelphia Inquirer,* really good guy and sportswriter. Made me smile to head out early in the morning thinking of that old story and those days.

I often think, especially in recent years, the pull for me out there on Standing Rock isn't only my conviction that there is something in Lakota culture that the world needs, but also that the country itself is sacred. All the world is, I'm sure, but there, for me at least, it seems to come through so clearly.

One thing that was part of the SD experience from very nearly the beginning was making the trip from Bullhead to the southern part of the state. This was essentially the pull of Wounded Knee. *Bury My Heart at Wounded Knee* and *Black Elk Speaks* were important books for me. I began reading these and other books relating to Indigenous American history that decade in my twenties when I was playing ball, especially the Oklahoma City years. It just seemed natural, looking back on it, poking around in bookstores in places like Wichita and Denver and Omaha to pick up those kinds of books. When our kids were growing up, I felt it was important to take them both, on separate trips, to Wounded Knee, important for them to learn that part of American history.

Initially, it was just that and the desire to hike to the top of what was then still called Harney Peak, now Black Elk Peak. I also liked to have lunch at Bette's Kitchen in Manderson. I didn't just like it—I thought it was practically an honor to have the opportunity. I still feel that way. Betty was the great-granddaughter of Black Elk. She passed in 2024. Her terrific small restaurant was in her home, on the site where Black Elk transcribed his Great Vision to John Neihardt.

In 2015 I made the drive from Standing Rock to Pine Ridge specifically to have lunch at Bette's. I took kind of the back way, through Wanbli, to avoid the outrageous fee to go through Badlands National Park for just a few miles to get to Manderson. As I crossed the White River, an eagle flew across in front of me. A few miles later I stopped to pick up an older guy hitchhiking. This is still an hour or so from Manderson. He'd hit a deer earlier that morning, disabling his truck. He asked where I was going and when I said Bette's Kitchen, he laughed and said he lived maybe a quarter mile south of it. He called his wife, who was planning to come get him, to tell her that he'd gotten a ride. It was funny to all of us, I think, to hear him say he'd been picked up by someone who just happened to be going to Bette's. Closest I ever came to a Field of Dreams moment. He invited me to come back the next year for a sweat, which I did, and we became friends. I am indebted to him in several ways. He introduced me to the Sweat Lodge. He showed me the "Spiritual Path," the route Crazy Horse's parents took to bring his body back to Pine Ridge after his death. He taught me to say "All my relations" at the end of a prayer.

Fast forward to 2023—somehow all this back story seems relevant to me—driving down for a one-day 600-mile round trip to have lunch at Bette's Kitchen, and then back to Standing Rock.

But I'd only thought of the strangeness of that old baseball story and 100,000 miles and now my old KIA and 200,000 miles right before I'd left home. There are a couple of different ways to make that 300-mile drive, and both of them are through what is to me hauntingly beautiful and empty country.

So as I was just getting started, still early morning, I was thinking about the note I'd sent to my kids—Man, that's progress and so on, and I began to think of a couple of other possible conclusions to come to about it. Stopped and wrote on the hood of my car this poem that just seemed to come with the whole scene. I really liked writing it, in that place in that moment, because it was all basically new to me except for the Man, that's progress. And I felt indebted to the sacred country all around.

All my relations.

WEALTH'S WAR!!!
BY:
©
2023

*17 December 2023*

## Wealth is War!

Wealth is War!
and billionaires are money addicts

My best friend died
in a meth house last year
he was one-thousandth as much

of a meth addict as bill the
gates is a money addict

and yet my friend is
dead and disrespected
and Bill Gates is alive

and on the evening news

There is a story to this poem and Gilbert Kills Pretty Enemy's design, but first: When you predict a sea-change is coming in the near future and some dozen years after the world doesn't look all that much different, you either need to offer some explanation or perhaps need to regroup a little bit.

Actually that part isn't too hard for me. Believe it or not, I still think I was right. There *was* something in the air that winter of 2007-08. It was, after all, when Obama's most unlikely Presidential campaign caught fire and resulted in his election.

Perhaps I was too young to fully appreciate the Civil Rights movement of the 60's, but for me Obama's election was the most important event in American history in my lifetime, and I am not embarrassed to say I shed tears of joy more than once during one or more of his speeches and on election night itself.

And as for the year 2011, two things happened that were exactly the kind of things I might have hoped for, spontaneous expressions of people around the world to bring about a better day—the Arab Spring and Occupy Wall Street.

Even at the end of Obama's second term, it was impossible for me just on a personal level not to be moved when the NODAPL movement on Standing Rock, where I had been going for nine summers in search of answers, received worldwide attention and recognition for making one simple, incredibly powerful statement to the world: "Water Is Life".

Now for the tragedy of the thing, at least from my point of view: It is the accuracy of my first vision that seems to have overwhelmed, so far, the power of my second. In other words, the depth, power, almost separate life-will of racism in our white hearts quite simply and most basically resulted in President Donald Trump.

"Now we are engaged in a great Civil War testing whether this nation..." just kidding, sort of, but if Donald Trump is President-elect on December 17th, 2024, it will be a cicada-cycle, a full haiku for my Vision of 2007 and I will...well, I don't know what I'll do. Just have to wait and see, I guess.

Now for the poem and design. In the summer of 2017, with a friend and my son, I started a little project in Bullhead in conjunction with the yearly V-J Day Celebration the second weekend in August that I called Old-Time Baseball. It was just the idea of doing something on Standing Rock that I knew a little about—playing ball with kids, or trying to getting kids playing ball on their own. We did free baseball and softball in the weekdays leading up to the Celebration, provided food and drink, left behind a lot of equipment, and so forth.

That first summer I met T. It was an auspicious morning for me when we met. I was with my son at a friend's house there in Bullhead getting ready to hike to Sitting Bull's camp a few miles away, the spot where Sitting Bull was born and where he was killed. It is a sacred place, in my view (I know—like all places on the earth), but in this case especially because Sitting Bull's death on the morning of December 15, 1890 started a chain of events that ended 300 miles away with the Wounded Knee Massacre on December 29.

I really enjoyed meeting T. He was someone I felt naturally comfortable talking with from the start. He had a degree in Environmental Science. This was in the immediate aftermath of the NODAPL events of the previous winter, and we talked at some length about that.

When we returned for the baseball project in the summer of 2018, T. and his wife were instrumental in helping us achieve whatever modest things we got done. The friendship deepened—I just liked the guy. I thought he was funny and intelligent and also empathetic, even kind.

The summer of 2019 I went by myself for the Old-Time Baseball efforts, earlier this time, in June, thinking it made more sense to try to get things rolling at the beginning of summer. I had finished seven weeks of chemo-radiation a few months before. I couldn't have done anything that summer without T. and his wife's guidance and help, along with another friend I'd made, Matthew Yellow Earrings.

For a number of reasons, I felt I could only make the one trip out to Standing Rock that summer. I missed the Celebration weekend for the first time since I'd started going out there in 2008. I talked with T. on the phone that Friday, the Opening Ceremony to begin that evening. They were staying in Fort Yates then, and I had sent a package with some small gifts to their Bullhead address. It was several days late. They knew it was coming and were in Bullhead for the start of the Celebration and called to touch base about the status of the package. I checked the tracking—it arrived the next day—and we talked things over for a little while.

Early the next evening T.'s wife called to tell me that he had died suddenly on their way home from the powwow the night before. One of those shocks of a lifetime. She talked at length in a tone of voice I will never forget—I believe the right term is "keening". Can't really discuss this further. It was pretty devastating.

Not long after that phone conversation I was hanging out in the garage, trying to come to grips. I have spent a lot of time there over more than 20 years, usually just thinking things over. And now, while I am not changing the title of my book, I had a third vision. It's a big garage and we leave the two overhead doors open year-round and in those 20+ years a lot of things have flown in and, usually , back out—birds and insects, of course. But on this night for the first time in my memory or experience a dragonfly flew in and bumped into the closed window pane next to me. I typically shepherd the birds and insects trapped this way back out to freedom. I realized not only that I had never caught or touched a dragonfly, but also that I'd had a fear of the darn things going back to childhood. At any rate, I caught this one easily. They are almost soft to the touch. As I walked to the open door to let it go, I looked at its face and as god is my witness, I saw T.'s face there. I let it go and as it flew off to the south, it was T.'s voice I heard quite clearly: Just let my spirit go, bro. People who knew him, if they can still remember, would recognize the intonation immediately—T!

Fast forward a year—the pandemic summer of 2020. The powwow was called off. The weekend powwow, or wacipi, is actually called the V-J Day Celebration, remembering, remarkably in this remote Native American village, the end of World War II and honoring Veterans of all wars. It was the 75th Anniversary of the end of the war and I got some money together, some letters of congratulations and support from people and organizations in baseball, some t-shirts and caps made, and so forth. We gave away these things in Matthew's driveway the Friday night the Celebration would have started. Very informal. It was also the first anniversary of T.'s passing, and I had a dozen or so t-shirts made with his name on them, in his memory.

In the middle of handing out the stuff, really just a fun and impromptu gathering, someone there felt it was important to tell me that T. had died in a meth house. The way this hit me is hard to describe—it basically just added a layer of sadness for me about his death. But also, being told in that way at that moment, I felt a kind of undercutting—were people looking at me all this time as some sort of an absurd person from outside doing dumb or meaningless things?

I also sponsored a radio broadcast the next day on KLND—the reservation radio station. This was to be a virtual powwow hosted by former tribal chairman Jay Taken Alive. The story of that broadcast is crucial to this whole thing but I am telling it elsewhere.

The point here is that sometime over the next year, mulling over the impact of the dragonfly vision, the revelation about T.'s death, the way I felt about our friendship, it hit me very powerfully: It's the greed, stupid. T. and I were simpatico. He was every bit as capable as any of my friends from high school and college who went on to great success, great material rewards, in their adult lives. Virtually every one of them. What hit me so clearly one night, again out there in the garage, was that the driving force behind my culture surrounding and suffocating T.s, the destruction of this continent and the people that had been living on it (Why did we steal all that land?), was plain and fucking simple: money, and hoarding it. The power that sees an ancient forest and thinks only of the money to be made cutting it down.

So I wrote the poem above and asked Gilbert Kills Pretty Enemy to make a design. We had to talk about it a bit. He said to me once—there's a lot of different kinds of wealth and I said—O no, I know—this is the kind of wealth that drives destruction, taking, taking, taking, and hoarding, and so forth.

Having a kind of Trump-figure pulling the strings, so to speak, was a stroke of genius, in my view at least. But the central idea for me, which I asked Gilbert about and he said—Yes, that's what I told you already—is that the design is a kind of medicine wheel gone wrong, with the four corners pitted against each other and the demonic center—greed—out of control, out of the center, and crazy-evil.

## 2026: The Reckoning

So as 2026 rolled in, one would think the whole Trump fiasco would be enough to make me face facts about this Vision of 2007. It turned out to be simpler than that. A friend called me out on this book: The Vision II part wasn't working. It took me a moment, but only a moment, to realize the problem at the heart of the matter is that the world has not become a better place as I foresaw. Duh.

So now I'm the most minor of prophets having to face the unavoidable fact: My vision failed. Actually, this may be the one thing I share with major or real prophets. As I understand it, Jesus and Paul and even Mohamed felt the change they preached or prophesied was going to happen in the immediate future. The first paragraph of *Moby-Dick* has been rattling around in my head the last few months. The followers of the real prophets create new religions. I, with no followers and doubtless deservedly so, take myself out to Standing Rock and write poems and hike to the top of Thunder Butte to pray.

Another fact I've been coming to grips with: I feel I know the exact crucial moment where not only my vision failed, but I failed it. It took me over a year and a trip out to SD to write the first part, the first essay, in "Intimations". I didn't really plan adding to it before 2011, each piece of writing just had a certain inevitability to it for me. Then I was astonished, frankly, in 2011 by first the Arab Spring and then Occupy Wall Street.

In the fall of 2011, I was 58 years old teaching school in Mio. I loved going to NYC in my younger years, am not unfamiliar with the city, and devised a plan to get to Zuccotti Park to be there at sunrise on October 23rd, my 59th birthday, to do a sound practice and just participate. Almost a personal celebration, you might say. As I remember that would have been a Friday (important in terms of making sub plans). Both our kids were living in other states. I asked a young former student, a friend of the family and an artist, to go with me.

My friend bailed and I got the flu that week and I just...couldn't get it together to make the trip. And then it seemed to me Occupy just dissolved, or went out with a whimper or whatever, at least as a physical presence in Manhattan. Black Elk blamed himself when the forces of history overwhelmed his Great Vision. And again as the most minor of figures comparing myself to a real visionary, I can't help but think if I'd only gotten out there....But the point is, aside from opening myself up to ridicule for even saying that, it is simply true that everything after that has been post-vision. The results are in, my vision failed.

Several times over the years I have talked with high school students about what I call the bowling-alley experience. Roll the ball as per usual, then take about two steps past the foul line, turn around and look back. Everything is different, beautifully so. I've had only one student try this and report back. It was the same for him

This is what it is like acknowledging that my vision failed (have I mentioned that yet?) and then looking back at the post-2011 experience and the writing about it.

Early in 2020 I got a little poem that seems not to have resonated with anyone I've shared it with but is crucially important to me. I call it Early Morning Poem—I woke up very early one winter morning and there it was, followed by a brief Kototama Manifesto. This is my Plato's Cave story, my secret, or real, life emerging from...however one wishes to view this world of human experience—darkness and chains works pretty well for me.

And I am coming to look at the last 15 years, basically, as what the meadowlark taught me: The way into this real world is through vision, the sharing of dreams, poems, and prayer. Perhaps only for the briefest of moments at a time. But still.

At the Celebration in 2019, I asked my friend Matthew one morning if he would be attending the festivities. He said he didn't care too much for the way the powwow is conducted these days. The traditional way was just to wake up in the morning, have some coffee, and dance. I couldn't let go of that and in 2021 we sponsored a sunrise dance at the Celebration. Matthew passed almost exactly a year ago but the sunrise dance has continued.

So in the here and now of Feb. 1, 2026, all I really have to do is get this book with Gilbert's art out in the world before the beginning of summer.

Then it will be just like the conclusion of my Baseball Enlightenment poem: 2 outs, bottom of the 9th, everything empty, facing the best relief pitcher in the league. Only I am not the guy striking out this time—I am the beer vendor at the edge of consciousness, hawking my wares like a motherfucker, selling my book with our signatures for $100, to raise $10,000 to have an afternoon of feasting and honoring Lakota elders and the

Lakota language and culture, awaking to a sunrise dance, with coffee, in the sacred morning.

And inviting the world to come.

# *Afterwords*

RED LIVES

ROCK

*2020*

## The Broadcast

The day after the giveaway in Matthew's driveway, we did a kind of virtual powwow broadcast at radio station KLND, the reservation station located a dozen or so miles from Bullhead. I had gotten to know station director John Brave Bull the year before. We talked quite a bit about what we might be able to do on the air to commemorate the 75th anniversary of the V-J Day Celebration. In a conference call with several people who worked at the station, Jay Taken Alive, a former tribal chairman, agreed to host, or emcee, the broadcast. I made a point of saying it was really important to me on a personal level to commemorate as well the one-year anniversary of T.'s passing, and how deeply I had been affected by that.

I was scheduled as a guest on the broadcast, the only one really, to talk of course about what I was doing and why. It's almost impossible for me to describe the way I was feeling that morning going into the broadcast after the news I had received the night before about T.'s passing. It wasn't just that I felt a new kind of sadness about his death, but also the way I was told—like it was important to know the circumstances of his death if I was going to go around passing out t-shirts with his name on them. I'd been going out to Standing Rock for a couple weeks a year for a dozen years, but it's not like I had deep roots, or roots of any kind really, in the community or the culture. T. was the best friend I'd made.

What I can say, then, is that it felt genuinely wonderful early on in the broadcast to hear Jay say we were also honoring the memory of their relative and my friend T. The first time he said it something just gave way inside me, in a good way. He repeated this in one way or another throughout the more than three-hour broadcast, and every time his words washed over me in a cleansing kind of way.

This made it easy, then, when they asked me to tell the story of coming out there for so many years and particularly the 75th Anniversary things to just relax and enjoy talking it over. This was a conversation with Mike Kills Pretty Enemy in the studio and Jay from his home because of COVID concerns.

It was interesting and even fun to tell the basic story that had meant so much to me for so long to a Lakota audience. Of course there was a particular focus on the V-J Day Celebration and the things we'd done related to that. I realized in the days before I got out there that if I were honestly to tell the truth about what I was doing that summer and why, the real story behind it, I would have to go all the way back to a dream I had in a motel room in North Dakota the night before I first got to Standing Rock in 2008. I talked with John Brave Bull the day before about this, not because it was such a long story but because I was uncertain all the content was ok for broadcast. I got specific about what I meant and John told me people had said worse on air, which wasn't all that reassuring, but he also pointed out that Lakota culture is a "dream culture", placing great importance on them.

I was still a little leery, and didn't get into that part of the story the first time I talked on air with Mike. I talked about my vision, humbly, and the sunrise at Sitting Bull's grave, and stumbling on and returning to the powwow for a dozen years, and starting the youth baseball/softball things. Then there was a break for a powwow song, which was the basic format for the whole broadcast. Intervals of talking followed by a powwow song or two, the songs following a typical powwow kind of sequence.

I admit this was a pleasure for me. And the sense of relief and joy I felt every time Jay said they were remembering and honoring their relative T. only added to it. Immeasurably. John came in during a song break to tell me to go for it, talk about the dream, so I did. This next part I am transcribing from a tape John sent me later. Partly because this may tell the story more directly than I could write it out now. But mainly I am coming to believe that how we share and act on powerful dreams is important in itself, so that this moment of talking about it on KLND is part of the story. It begins with Mike Kills Pretty Enemy encouraging me in a thinly-veiled way to talk about the dream.

Mike: You were mentioning or talking with the other John yesterday about a more specific item that was part of your focus about being here in the Standing Rock area. Let us know about that.

JP: Well, ok, sure

*(Then I summarized in a couple minutes what I had already touched on earlier, what appears at the beginning of Part 2 of this book: the phone call from a former student then stationed with the Army in Germany, the resulting "vision" about 2011, and the strong sense that December night in 2007 that the world was going to change for the better.)*

JP: The tugging at the edge thing that I didn't understand was that the change was somehow going to come from South Dakota. So that's why I came out in August of 2008. It's kind of funny—I was being cagey about it, or humble, or something—I decided to sort of sneak up on South Dakota, go to North Dakota first and maybe poke around there a little bit.

I was looking for the most off-the-beaten path way, not dirt roads—two-lane highways, to get here, and I wound up in Linton (North Dakota) at the end of the first day. I pretty quickly figured out it probably seemed the most off-the-beaten path because it's 35 miles in either direction to get across the Missouri River.

I was looking at the map (I still use a road atlas instead of GPS) and there was Standing Rock on the other side of the river, basically off to the southwest. I know I had travelled through that country before, and no doubt seen the signs, but I wasn't as familiar with Standing Rock as I was with other reservation names like Pine Ridge and Rosebud.

I was the only person staying at this little motel and I asked the owner, What about the Indian reservation on the other side of the river? I was thinking about going there.

And he said (*laughing a little*)—this isn't funny, really. Why would you want to go there? They would scalp you except you don't have any hair.

I call that a double-dis. He was disrespecting with a negative stereotype Native Americans and disrespecting me because I'm bald, which I thought was a little nervy of him since I was the only person staying at his motel.

Anyhow, when I went to bed I was still debating which way to go, up to Bismarck and across the river with this North Dakota idea I had, or south.

I woke up in the middle of the night and there was a thunderstorm, coming very clearly from the southwest, from South Dakota. So I said to myself, Well, it looks like I'm going to South Dakota and right at that instant there was a really big thunderclap, and I said, Well, I'm going to South Dakota, and fell back asleep.

And then I had this dream. I don't have a particular philosophy or knowledge about dreams but I've had a dozen or so that just seemed important. I don't need to have ideas about them, they're powerful enough for me on their own and this was one of those dreams..

OK—so in my dream I was taken back home—to my family. It wasn't the house we were living in but sort of an amalgam of all the houses my wife and I have lived in over the years. Our kids were there, and other members of the family.

They were like—especially my daughter—What are you doing in North Dakota? You said your vision was South Dakota. What are you doing?

And I said, Well, I am in North Dakota—I was being sneaky about it—but tomorrow I'll be in South Dakota. It sounded really stupid to me even as I was saying it.

And then it seemed that my grandmother was there, who lived to be 98 but had passed away 15 years before. And I felt confused for a moment and I said—her name is Isabel—Is Grandma Isie still alive? She was a strong woman but she was frail, of course, in her 90's. We had a large dog, and I was afraid of the dog accidentally hurting her.

And so it turned out that it was Grandma Isie and she wasn't very old and frail but actually a little girl. I recognized her very clearly even though she had a lot of freckles, almost speckled, which I don't think she ever had in real life. So this is the part I asked John about, talking about this yesterday. My grandmother was a kind and religious and gentle woman, and I don't think I ever heard her utter a swear word, but she also grew up on a farm in Ohio in the late 1800's and she could be a strong, plain-spoken woman when the time was right.

So with that buildup (Gosh, this makes me laugh) my daughter walked over with her, and my daughter said to me: Isie wants to know how it is you can twitch your nose and feel it in your nuts.

I just thought that was so funny. It was kind of like how in the world do I take myself so seriously with this vision, driving 1000 miles, and it was as big a deal probably as Elizabeth Montgomery in Bewitched twitching her nose and.... There were just these different sides to it, all making me laugh.

I woke up chuckling. I was chuckling all the way down to South Dakota and what added to it just a few miles out of town—if I'd gone north I wouldn't have seen it—there was a sign: Birthplace of Lawrence Welk. Both my grandmothers loved Lawrence Welk. Of course I was at an age then, my older brother and sister and I—it wasn't like the 60's, we weren't hippies, it was like crew-cut nerds making fun of Lawrence Welk.

OK—so I found the place, found a place to watch the sunrise, but the first person I talked to on Standing Rock was in McLaughlin. I was sitting in my car in front of the Prairie Dog Café, and Glenn Looking Horse came over to talk to me. Everybody I've asked in Bullhead knows Glenn and mentions his nickname, which I can never remember, but at any rate we had a really pleasant conversation for about 10 minutes. I said to him at one point—and if I hadn't had that dream, I'm sure I wouldn't have mentioned this—but I said to him just kind of in passing: I drove by Lawrence Welk's birthplace this morning, and don't say anything bad about Lawrence Welk because both my grandmothers loved him.

And Glenn said, Yeah, black and white TV. And I said, What? and he said, Black and white TV.

And it was like when you look at a tree and you see there's an unusual shape, and you're not sure if it's a bird, or an animal, or just a strange configuration of branches. I said What? again, and he said, with real emphasis this time, Black and White TV!

And it was like—a bird taking wing—it just exploded into life for me, where what he meant was that the Black and White culture I had come from, not just Lawrence Welk white-bread culture but everything, soul music coming into my childhood from Motown—from Detroit just 100 miles away—everything was Black and White TV and was missing something. And that—this thing that was missing as I sat in the powwow year after year I came to think is color, and most specifically red, blood, you know, life, a full human life—and where we are now, my culture, maybe the whole world, where we are now is like Black and White TV compared to what our potential is.

That's why really the story of my journey here is just as simple as...You know I made t-shirts to give away yesterday and most of them were V-J Day Celebration t-shirts with a medicine wheel image. But I made a few, and I was pleased that people liked them—that said Red Lives Rock. You know, Standing Rock. And the idea of that is going from Black and White TV to Red Lives Rock.

I just thought of that idea for a t-shirt a few weeks ago at the height of the Black Lives Matter protests—the reaction to the George Floyd killing. I was heartened to see people in my country, my culture, my white brothers and sisters, that spontaneous reaction and waking up, it seemed to me.

But one thing that sort of gnawed at me was to say—and I know the way that people intend it—the way we say that racism and slavery is our original sin in America. It's really not going back to our original sin on this continent—the destruction and decimation of Native American people and cultures and often the continent itself. This is really the bedrock of what's gone wrong.

But also strangely enough—and the Bible is important to me although I don't belong to any church—the first or deepest meaning of it, Red

Lives Rock, was a religious one. Like Jesus saying to Peter: You're the rock of the Christian church.

And I was thinking that the spirit that I'm talking about—there's something here that is necessary, and I thought the real rock or foundation for the world is involved with this spirit that's in Native American culture. Red Lives is the Rock, so to speak. That's the way I took it. I think it *is* as simple as going from Black and White TV to Red Lives Rock over the years that I have come here.

Sometimes you just have to say it: This was a good, big day for me. To get this out, these things I had been thinking and feeling and dreaming about for more than a dozen years, in the place that all of that had brought me to, to be welcomed into this studio, and have this conversation, and frankly—in Jay's later commentary—to be honored for sharing my vision and dream, and to have my friend's life, however tragically it had ended, honored as well—a great day.

## And Finally...Prayer

### The Snake

Two secrets I've held close to my heart
one I've forgotten,
the other is this:

Out back by the old chicken coop
I killed a harmless garter snake
    on accident
curious about its diet and past,
I opened up its belly
and was shocked to see
seven babies there inside
now outside—
        a snake slaughter

But of all things this:
one lone snake raised its
head and breathed, just once

And I felt the soul enter its body,
and I felt the universe shudder,
and the rise and fall of my own soul—
my own single-breath glimpse
        of eternity

Earlier in this book I wrote that a single line of poetry was my philosophy of life. After this experience, I realized I had a philosophy of the soul—because I had felt it: the soul enters the body with the first breath.

It wasn't just this one moment, of course. I attended three home births in the 80's, two of them our own children. It's a little bit of a story, but I "delivered" (caught is a better term, in my experience) two of the babies as they arrived in the world. There is a profound silence, unlike anything else. And then with the first breath, a new universe is created, or so it seemed to me.

I found that the biggest impact of this moment—feeling that the soul really and truly does enter with the first breath—was to give me a new seriousness about the next part of breathing, the exhalation, and particularly in the exhalation the articulation of human sound. To me it meant there *is* an intrinsic sacredness to speech. We don't have to make up ideas about it over the centuries, some philosophy derived from thinking about it.

And I say again, because it's fun to say, I really agree with Jesus on this one, from the Gospel of Thomas: "For what goes into your mouth will not defile you, but that which issues from your mouth —it is that which will defile you."

I wrote the poem about the snake in early 2017 shortly after coming home from a hospital stay. I had fairly recently gotten into the habit then of referring to the sound practice as prayer. For instance, in October of 2016, I wrote to the President that I went to the NODAPL camp primarily because I wanted to pray there at sunrise on my birthday—October 23rd. I was referring to the sound practice. But the reason I used the term prayer in this way was simply that my exposure to Lakota culture, especially sitting in the powwow stands over the years, had expanded my definition of what prayer might be.

It seems I just needed this little nudge—and perhaps the crucial moment was actually writing down: I felt the soul enter its body—to genuinely consider the sound practice to be prayer.

In this I am also grateful for a period of time some 20 years earlier when I had experimented with saying The Lord's Prayer daily with all the attention and focus I could muster. I typically spoke it quietly, just in my room—it doesn't take long—but out loud.

It was interesting. The most important thing to me is I found over time it began to resonate over the rest of the day, not so much as conscious thought but just a kind of foundation for approaching or even receiving the things of daily life. One small example: If you say in a prayerful manner, out loud and day after day, "Give us this day our daily bread", over time you realize, or at least I did, that a really wealthy person just can't do it, not without a sense of irony coming through, and it doesn't seem to me a prayer where irony works. So that—and not to take a cheap shot, but sincerely— "Billionaire Christian" seems to me a contradiction in terms. I'd leave it up to individual millionaire Christians to search their souls about how sincerely they can pray, Give us this day our daily bread.

Then there was a kind of cascading effect I have been trying to write about and understand for nearly seven years now, relating this sense of prayer to the sound practice. The importance of the sound practice is its resonance or impact on the rest of our daily life, and this impact is harder to get a handle on as the sound practice is not really in the language of our daily life.

And what is the impact? Years ago I described it simply as "More life". This part I didn't get more fully until I came into my "taxonomy" of consciousness a couple years ago, thanks to a dying meadowlark. In a human culture where the physical sense experience and the knowledge and thought naturally accompanying is dominant, it is prayer, specifically for me the Kototama sound practice as I learned it from Hikalu, that opens us up to other human capacities, for me caught in visions, dreams, and poems.

What is hidden or covered over is often forgotten, sooner or later. I believe there are innate human capacities that we feel in varying measures simply because we are born, and breathe, and speak. In our world, our civilization, our culture, these capacities, I would say, are actively denigrated and denied.

I'm not sure if I've ever mentioned this before, but my idea of the way to reconnect with the full range of human capacity is to get yourself out in a meadow somewhere and...

# Appendix

1. New Group

As I wrote at the outset, I considered the two "visions" upon which this book is based to actually be visions, however humble, in part because I stand by the validity of the conclusions they led me to: we still haven't understood or acknowledged our racist past and present, which means we are powerless, in my view, to fully move forward from it. And there is something in Lakota culture the world needs.

It is also important to me to have acted, in the real world, in some way in response. This needs to be something more, in my opinion, than just writing or talking about them. On Standing Rock I have sponsored and led youth baseball/softball activities. I've done some things regarding the V-J Day Celebration over the years—these are humble activities in both scope and impact, but the point is I tried.

It took me almost five years to get the Donnie Moore essay written. But I talked about his death, the impact it had on me, why it impacted me so powerfully and so forth from the moment it happened. It is also important to me that immediately in the aftermath I tried to do something in the world, the effort forming what I called or hoped would be a New Group. The summary of its goals and methods are included below in the pamphlet I put together.

There were two basic ideas here: one is that a great perpetuating mechanism of racism has next to nothing to do directly with black people. It is the way white people talk amongst ourselves, if you will, when no black people are around. We don't call each other out, in my experience, when someone uses a racial slur. Of course we don't if "we" is a Klan meeting. But those are actually quite rare, I believe, and far more often it is true that among groups of relative strangers, the most racist person in the room has felt comfortable venting with one kind of pejorative comment or another. In my experience, these are almost always met at most with a supposedly disapproving silence. I'm embarrassed about this personally, but I also understand it to some degree. Its not just that like many sane and reasonable people I dislike confrontation. But also I think its no coincidence that the most racist person in the room is usually the one most prone to violence. I honestly don't know in this case if it is cowardice, but I was just never a guy ready to get in a fight about this at the drop of a hat.

So I wanted a way to get proactive about this matter, and the second basic idea of my little project I stole from another kind of campaign. I thought the old bumper stickers that used to be quite common: "Warning—I brake for animals" were genius. On the face of it, they were just a safety warning about the driver's perhaps not universal driving practice. But it was also a great statement, I thought, about the importance the driver attached to the matter, and in that way, a really great non-confrontational argument for their position. And the more prevalent the bumper stickers became, the more I thought they had an impact on all drivers. What I mean is at some level almost no one likes to be thought a jerk, and I thought it was at least possible a lot of people might become more vigilant about their driving in this regard.

That's what I wanted my little lapel pins to do. If enough people wore them and enough people asked about them, the argument about not offending others with racial slurs would be made pretty effectively before the slurs happened .

Or so I thought. I was living in Boulder then, a great place to find an artist to make lapel pins. I found Bruce Teschner to make mine. In 1990 I formally got non-profit status for the one and only time in my life—so far—and this was the result:

New Group

We are forming a new group. Our purpose is to oppose bigotry in all its forms.

Our activity is wearing a simple gold circle lapel pin. If people ask us about it, we intend to say it means we don't appreciate hearing racist, ethnic, or sexist comments, slurs, or jokes.

Our intent in this is to make a positive contribution to the ongoing dialogue in our community about the problems of prejudice. We believe that unless the community is actively engaged in discussing these issues, the resulting silence and indifference act as a kind of support mechanism for intolerance.

The pin means only what the wearer intends it to mean. We are not the arbiters of what is or is not appropriate behavior. We are too painfully aware of our own shortcomings in viewing all individuals without prejudice to adopt that approach. In fact, we believe one of the advantages of wearing this pin is that it will make us more sensitive to these shortcomings in ourselves.

There are several things we like about this activity. It is a statement we can make daily about the importance of the problem. It is peacefully assertive. And it offers an opportunity for people to engage in a cooperative activity on a completely democratic basis. We are a group without leaders or, to put it another way, anyone who wears our pin with a good spirit is one of our most important leaders.

We hope these ideas strike a chord with you. The pins cost $15 apiece. The logo on the front of this brochure is a representation of the pin's design. They have been designed and made by a local artist and are approximately the size of a nickel. For comments, pin orders, or more information about us, write to:

New Group
1531 Broadway
Boulder, CO

2. Haiku years

As I wrote earlier, my basic literary output for a couple years was just a few haikus. Here they are. Most of the ones from 2016 had titles, which I don't think are allowed. Whatever, but I have dropped them here. One title in particular I liked—"Vertebrae: A concrete haiku for Hikalu", especially since Hikalu was a concrete poet and artist himself of some note in NYC in the 60's and early 70's. But as the title would almost be a new haiku itself, in fact would be if I simply included his birth name, Carl Fernbach Flarsheim, it seems best to leave it out.

2015

If you want to be
consider the seasons and
dwell in the words

2016

Drove to Ohio,
listening to Mahler's 4th,
gave a baseball talk

delineated
bones, stones, I mean notes, amen
tones, a sonnet, me

Do I remember
Her voice? Her voice is the pond
Upon which I skate

I am a mystic
Frogs are really croaking now
Summer pretty old

At least in one sense
I won. This fall Clay's photo
In the trophy case

We are racing to
Oblivion or ecstasy
Old in October

Leaves falling one by
One. Even Jesus was in
Despair on the cross

On a wintry night
in Michigan—same old song:
Honor your daily life

3. NODAPL

It also feels appropriate to include here from 2016 something from my brief stay at the NODAPL camp in October of 2016. I thought that was a remarkable camp, a remarkable movement. Not writing at length about that here. Just two things. There was a central meeting place for the camp, a continual fire, meetings of one kind or another going on virtually all the time I was there. I was just walking by at one point late afternoon, catching what I could of an elder's speech, and I won't forget one thing he said: "Our Mother Earth is sick now; she needs our help". It wasn't just the content, which alone is a beautiful and succinct and powerful statement, but also the intonation. It was simply just about the most sincere, heartfelt statement I've ever heard a human voice make, filled with pain and yet also somehow hope.

Then also just want to include this letter to Barack Obama about my experience there. Published this also in Good Ol' Daily Kos.

10/27/2016

Dear President Obama,

Last night I listened to a North Dakota police official say he is losing patience with the Dakota Access protesters now occupying the easement for the pipeline. He said the "rule of law" must be upheld.

I don't think he saw any irony in saying this to Indian people. Of course if this nation were genuinely about the rule of law, the Black Hills would be returned to the Lakota people tomorrow. Except they wouldn't have been stolen in the first place. There wouldn't be a vacancy on the Supreme Court today. Corporations wouldn't be considered to be people. Money wouldn't be free speech. Presidential candidates wouldn't say they may or may not accept the results of an election. And so on.

I drove 1000 miles last Friday and Saturday to camp at the protest site near Cannon Ball. I had an intense desire to pray there at sunrise on the 23rd, my 64th birthday. This was personal for me on several levels. I'd had a similar desire to be at the Occupy Wall Street camp five years earlier, not because I thought my personal presence would be important in any way, but because I wanted to link my personal experience to what I thought was the best part of my culture trying to change things from the inside. Not long after that the Occupy movement, it seemed to me, was simply crushed. It left its mark, but things haven't changed.

Also, I have been going out to the Standing Rock Reservation every year since 2008, attending portions of the Rock Creek Powwow held in Bullhead, South Dakota. Bullhead is named for the Indian police officer who shot and killed Sitting Bull before being shot and killed himself. This happened on the Grand River, not far from the present site of the village, on December 15th, 1890. It started a series of events which culminated at Wounded Knee on the 29th.

Despite going out there for years I claim no personal connection with the people or culture of Standing Rock. I simply believe it is sacred country and that the Lakota people have something that is sacred as well.

So on the morning of the 23rd, well before sunrise, the camp was awakened by a leader calling over the loudspeakers for the people to rise up and act. 81 people had been arrested the day before. Over the next couple hours there were prayers and songs and speeches, mainly intimating that this was an important day for the movement and a day of change.

Some time after first light we headed off to the site of the pipeline. Some drove there. I walked with a group of, I would guess, 200 or so. A plane had been flying over the camp before we left and it was now joined by a helicopter circling over us.

When we got to the site there was an extended period of singing and praying. Then a speaker said that this was the day to take a stand, to make a camp on the easement itself. This was electrifying to me. Occupy Wall Street never got past occupying a small park in the shadow of the skyscrapers. It was also criticized for not having a specific goal. Now the Dakota Access movement would be occupying the proposed pipeline site itself. And I don't think its basic position could be more clear: Water is life.

I don't know if the people camping on the site now are willing to sacrifice their lives before moving, but I believe that would be a righteous position to take. I don't think this is about the rule of law. I don't even think it is about the few billions of dollars involved. There are individual Americans who could buy off the whole project to date and not even feel it financially. I believe it is about whether or not in 2016 we are willing to honestly look at and change our relationship with the earth and each other.

I count myself among your biggest admirers. I hope and pray you will do something to honor the values and goals of the people of Standing Rock.

John Poff,
Mio, MI

**John Poff** is an old ballplayer, a semi-retired old schoolteacher, and was a licensed acupuncturist, practicing for a decade in the latter portion of the last century.

www.ingramcontent.com/pod-product-compliance
Lightning Source LLC
LaVergne TN
LVHW010853110826
845149LV00005B/1395

* 9 7 8 1 9 6 6 3 6 0 1 4 8 *